A Life Outside

Rock Climbing, Mountain Biking, and Other Outdoor Stories

Matt Artz

October 2007

First Edition

ISBN 978-0-6151-7240-8

For Sierra

(1989 - 2003)

Contents

Non-Fiction

My Cards on the Table
A Spring Solo of Table Mountain

The first piece of outdoor prose I ever wrote, this article previously appeared in Issue #1 (Summer 1999) of FunPig magazine.

Mountaineering is like religion. Many people just don't understand it. Of those who think they do understand it, each understands it differently. And the goals of religion and climbing are also similar. Everyone is looking for answers, for guidance, for Bhudda called "enlightenment," or what Steve Martin referred to as his "special purpose"...

Planning a climb of the Mountaineer's Route on Mt. Whitney in late July, I felt horribly inadequate. Having previously been only as high as 10,800 feet in elevation—a far cry from Whitney's 14,494 feet—surely the elevation would kill me if rock fall did not. Conditioning hikes up several peaks (Sugarloaf Peak, Mt. San Antonio, Mt. Harwood, West Baldy, Bighorn Peak) in Southern California's San Gabriel Mountains occupied the weekends. While these hikes were good for exercising and conditioning my body, these peaks were relatively low as well as relatively "safe." So I planned a trip to the Eastern Sierra to train, for the elevation and the exposure.

The plan was for my partner and I to climb Hurd Peak, 12,219 feet above sea level near Bishop in the Eastern Sierra Nevada Mountains. It was a fairly easy climb (a 2,500 gain from the trail head at South Lake), access was easy, and although there would still be some snow on the ground, most of it would be gone. After all, it was May. It was practically summer.

Then I got some bad news: Hurd Peak was unreachable because of heavy snow.

Fine, we would still go up to the Sierra, and look around for a peak that wasn't snowed in. There were plenty to choose from. We would probably just have to choose something at a slightly lower elevation.

Then I got some more bad news: my partner had to cancel.

O.K., maybe mountaineering was out of the question. I would take my mountain bike instead. That wouldn't be so bad. I could still get a great workout at elevation. Climbing shoes and chalk bag as well; I would be close to The Buttermilks, and could mountain bike over there for some hard-core bouldering.

Then I got some more bad news. It was raining and snowing heavily in the Sierra, and the forecast was for more of the same all weekend. The dirt roads were covered with snow and mud, so the mountain bike was out. The rocks were wet, so bouldering was out too.

Hmmm...oh, well, I still wanted to go to the Eastern Sierra. So I would just sit in the tent for a few days reading and resting. That wouldn't be so bad...

On the afternoon of May 6, 1994, I pulled in to Bishop Park Campground, elevation 8,200 feet, and was immediately taken by the enormity of the mountain across the road. Unlike the "typical" Eastern Sierra peak, which can be described as sharp and rocky and relatively compact, this mountain was massive and rounded, the flat top extending for miles with more than half a dozen separate knobby summits.

A quick look at the map showed that this was Table Mountain. The two summits directly across from me were 10,505 and 10,574 feet high; to the right were two higher knobs, at 11,200 and 11,286. The true highest point of this "mountain," being 11,711 feet and approximately two miles south, was not even visible from my vantage point. Peak 10,574 was looking like a very real possibility. There appeared to be several fairly straightforward routes up scree and gravel slopes to the right. Only a few moments of deliberation were necessary. It would be Peak 10,574 in the morning.

To some, climbing isn't as much a sport as it is a religion, and for them it takes the place of some other organized type of worship. The wilderness is the climbers' church, the mountain his sermon. His collection of gear, techniques, and knowledge is his bible. When distilled down to their most elemental forms, the main difference between the two religions is that the traditional worshipper is worried more about an afterlife, while a climber is preoccupied or even obsessed by death.

May 7, 1994, 6 a.m. I awoke late because it had been a bitterly cold and snowing off and on all night. My internal alarm clock was telling me to sleep in for a while longer. Surely there was no use in waking up early; my talus and scree route up the side of Peak 10,574 must be covered with at least two feet of fresh powder.

Within five minutes of waking, and without even peeking out the tent flap, I had decided to give it a try. What harm could it do? I would get cold and wet, turn back in 20 or 30 minutes, and at least have some pleasant memories of the aftermath of a beautiful Sierra storm. Then I could spend the rest of the day in the tent, reading and sleeping, but only a little disappointed, knowing I had at least given it a shot.

Double socks, separated by plastic bags so the feet would at least stay dry for a while in my lightweight summer hiking boots. Heavy pants, covered by rain pants. T-shirt, covered by a heavy sweater, topped off by a Gore-Tex jacket. Gloves covered by Gore-Tex mittens. Balaclava. In the 30-pound backpack, a stove, a tea kettle, two quarts of water, numerous Power Bars, a storm kit, an ice axe, helmet, ski poles, crampons, dry clothing, and enough other equipment and supplies to (hopefully) keep me safe, no matter what happened.

At 6:35 a.m., feeling (and undoubtedly looking) like some swollen victim of a bad allergic reaction, I clumsily stepped out of the tent. The scene was stunning. To a sightseer, the view would have been unbelievably beautiful; to me, daunted by the task ahead of me, it was a mixture of the sheer beauty and the stark reality that I intended to climb in these conditions!

Munching the last bagel not either stolen or partially eaten by the presumably rabid campground chipmunks, I set out across the road and dropped down to a peaceful marshy area where the previous afternoon I had spooked some mallard ducks. This morning there were no ducks; in fact, no signs of life at all, just snow. And it was still snowing, ever so lightly. Skirting the marsh to avoid an unpleasant dunking, I picked up a rough trail through some aspens on the right. I meandered through trees, out on to sage-covered flats, around and over rocky knobs, and then dropped steeply into a small canyon. The far side was an interesting, overhanging cliff about 35 feet high. This would be a great place to come back in the summer and rock climb, I thought, but right now it was just an ugly barrier barring any further progress. Luckily, it was not as bad a couple of hundred feet to the left, but it was covered with fallen trees and small branches that made it almost impenetrable. After some thrashing and wasted energy, I emerged on the plateau. This had to be the emotional low of the whole trip. Nothing beats thrashing about in near-impenetrable vegetation to make you feel like the biggest idiot who ever put on a pair of hiking boots.

A few minutes later I was at the edge of the talus slope that began the ascent of Peak 10,574—my peak for the day. The first few hundred feet were pretty bad. A few inches of fresh, wet snow covered the talus—just enough to hide the underlying rocks, but not enough to support any body weight over them. In a word, it just plain sucked.

After that, it only got worse. There was plenty of slipping and sliding to be had that morning on the slopes of Table Mountain! My goal became not to make it to the top of Peak 10,574, but to make it just a couple of hundred more feet to the cut of an abandoned mining road that traversed the side of the mountain.

Having gained the road after much thrashing, it was decision time. And the decision was simple. Another 1,500 feet or so on this snow-covered talus and scree would not be possible.

Maybe it was time to head back to the tent. Or maybe I could just follow the mining road for a while and see where it went.

The road went to the right for a quarter mile or so, where it crossed Jawbone Canyon. This canyon separates the two main flanks of Table Mountain. To the left (north), the two highest points were Peak 10,505 and Peak 10,574. To the right (south), a long plateau speckled with perhaps a dozen or more rocky knobs reaching more than 11,000 feet. Jawbone Canyon curves around and points directly towards the very shallow saddle between Peak 11,200 and Peak 11,286, the north most two of these knobs.

Up the canyon I went, towards the saddle, my intent being to break off to the left at about 10,000 feet and ascend the (hopefully) more consolidated slopes up to the top of Peak 10,574. For the first thousand feet or so the easiest way up was right up the center of the canyon, often suspended a few feet above the trickling stream below by a tongue of ice covered by snow. When conditions changed and the ice bridge began to give way at regular intervals of every 12 to 15 steps, my route tended to follow the break line between the stream bed and the adjacent slope.

It got steeper. And the snow got deeper. Place ice ax with right hand. Bite snow with ski pole in left hand. Move up with feet. Take a deep breath or two. Repeat ten times. Stop and collapse on the ski pole for a minute. Then repeat the whole process. It seemed like very slow going, but glancing at my watch I noticed I was actually making excellent time.

Whenever a boot broke through the thin crust of snow a few inches below the surface and sent my leg shooting down two feet into the snow, I would swing my ski pole back and make a large arc in the snow. This, I reasoned, would allow me to spot and avoid the weak spots in the snow on the way back down. It was a great idea...

The slope was getting ever steeper, and soon I stopped to stow the ski pole in my pack. It was just boots and ice axe from here on up. Judging from the map and the slight easing of the angle on the slope above me, it was only another two hundred feet or so to the summit of Peak 11,200.

Then an odd thing happened. The muscles in my left thigh began to cramp, first moderately and within a few minutes so intensely that I was hobbling along the steep slope towards the summit. As the slope suddenly lessened, I dropped my backpack and continued on, across a near-level plateau that rose gently to the top of Peak 11,200. Although the snow on this plateau was iced over and very crusty—the first non-powder encountered so far on the journey—I judged that with the short distance to the summit and the very kind slope, the effort to go back to the pack and put on crampons was not worth it. A few seconds later, I was on top.

The view was wonderful, but what should have been a delightful experience at the culmination of a long journey was of course overpowered by unfinished business—the ruggedly beautiful older sister, Peak 11,286. Her features were sharply defined, bold rocky outcrops juxtaposed against the softness of the fresh powdery snow and white wisps of low clouds. A natural beauty.

My visit with the little sister lasted less than a minute. I thought about turning back to the comfort of my tent, leaving my loftier goal for another day. Deliberation took about two seconds. It just wouldn't be right, after all that work. And it was so close, literally a couple of hundred yards and about 75 vertical feet away. Big sister was calling. She had more to offer.

The route over involved a descent of maybe a dozen feet to a large and almost indistinguishable saddle. Again, the ice was very slippery, but slow going and careful foot placement easily tamed it. Steering clear of an imposing icy cornice to the left, the traverse quickly dumped me at the base of the summit. The crusty ice instantly changed to fresh powder, about four feet deep. Picking my way through twisted trees and over large chunks of exposed rock, I gained the summit blocks. Success. Confirmation. Redemption.

Like religion, climbing can be a tricky thing. You know that when you die, the answers to all your questions will finally be answered. The tricky thing, the part you're after, is that you want to know the answers *now*. To get the answers, you must tempt death. It's like Halloween, except you want what you can't have — the trick *and* the treat.

Looking at my watch, it was 10:35 a.m., four hours to the minute after leaving camp. It was snowing lightly, as it had been for most of the morning. Balancing precariously on the icy summit blocks of Peak 11,286, the view was absolutely incredible. In front of me, I could look down into the valley where I had started. To the left was a virtual winter wonderland, the Table Mountain plateau stretching for a mile or two, dozens of miniature peaks topped with powdered sugar. To the right, Peak 10,574, my original goal, looked small, tame, and insignificant.

Then I looked behind me.

My route up looked steep and wild, true testimony to the adventure that had just transpired. Not small, nor tame, nor insignificant. Then it happened so quickly that it was like a dream. One second I was admiring the beauty of the steep chute that had been my stairway to heaven. The next moment I was in whiteout conditions, being pelted by heavy snowfall. Imagine looking down an elevator shaft and watching the elevator car come up, straight towards you, the roof painted white. Then imagine it suddenly ramming into your head with the force of a large piece of cold steel.

Things couldn't get any worse...or could they? I spent two, maybe three minutes on the summit. Running down the slope to regain my backpack, my left thigh started giving me problems again. Then the right joined in for a stereophonic symphony of pain. Getting to the pack was hard; going further was hell. I'd limp a few steps then collapse in the snow. Getting up was easy; it was the walking that was hard. I tried glissading a few times, but the snow was too deep and soft. Time to evaluate the situation.

Going on like I had been was no longer an option. No amount of will power or adrenaline would unlock the vice grips on my leg muscles. I spied a mangled tree where I could hunker down in a forced bivouac. Put on all the clothes I had, cover myself with my emergency space blanket, pull out the stove and start brewing tea.. I could survive for a while. But would people eventually start searching for me? I doubted they would find me. I was a couple of peaks away from where I had told people I was going. My footprints up Jawbone Canyon were already obliterated by the new snowfall. I was on the back side of the mountain, invisible from the road.

Gaining a summit is only 49% of the climb, a wise mountaineer once told me. In other words, 51% of the work was still ahead of me. But I was beginning to think that maybe 99% of the work was still ahead of me.

While evaluating my limited options and searching for the perfect bivouac site on the sparsely vegetated slope, my tight grip on my legs suddenly loosened ever so slightly. It was still extremely painful to move, but it was at least becoming possible now. Then I had a brainstorm. It was time to take the express elevator down Jawbone Canyon.

I had remembered a still unused feature of my new backpack. The padded area between my back and the backpack was removable, a little pad to sit on after a long day of hiking. "I'll never use that," I had thought when purchasing the pack. But here I was, in a raging snowstorm at 11,000 feet, trying to figure out how to remove the pad.

It came out easily, and unfolded into a 19-inch by 19-inch pad. Sitting on the pad and grasping the leading edge of it with my left hand, I laid my ski pole across my lap and firmly grasping my ice ax with my right hand placed it behind me for use as a brake. My legs were two stiff boards sticking straight out in front of my seated body. Completely useless, but at least no longer painful in this position.

The next 10 or 15 minutes was a blur of excited screams and flying powder. After what must have been at least 1,500 feet of elevation loss, the slope lessened and more rock began showing through the snow. But the improvised sled had done its job. I had gotten down the steepest, hardest part of the climb safely and quickly. And the brief rest had restored all energy to my legs, which now showed absolutely no signs of the debilitating cramps that had so severely threatened my retreat only half an hour before.

The rest of the hike out was uneventful. Fresh snow had completely obliterated my line of ascent and my carefully marked weak spots in the snow, but the surface had somewhat consolidated from the increasingly cold temperature, so it didn't matter. After a while, the snow turned to rain, which almost gave the impression of a warm shower even though the real temperature of the falling water was only a few degrees above freezing. Taking a more direct route towards the road, I avoided the most annoying parts experienced on the trip up.

Camp was a welcome sight. The cheap, uncomfortable folding chair looked like nirvana. Glancing at my watch, it was only 12:05 p.m. Unbelievably, my adventure had transpired in only five and a half hours. Time to sit down, drink a beer, and eat a ham sandwich. Life was good.

Back at camp, I quickly changed into dry clothes, made my sandwich, and opened "warm" (i.e., not quite yet frozen solid) beer. It was snowing on me, but I didn't care. I was hungry, and definitely used to the conditions. A few minutes later, I crawled into the tent, but the warmth of my -20 sleeping bag and tent was too much. Of course, the adrenaline was still pumping from the events of the day. Instead of sleeping, I began reading the first chapter in *Mountains of the Great Blue Dream* by Robert Leonard Reid.

> "Mountaineers climb because they love the mountains, yes; but they climb too because climbing prepares them boldly and tenaciously for death, then guides them faithfully to the edge of another world, a world I now recognize as the world of the dead, and there allows them to dance, mountain after mountain, year after year, as close to death as it is possible to dance; which is to say, within a single step. They go, not to die—that is very important—but far from the tumult of the valley below to linger in safe communion with death, to feel the exquisite tension that separates it from life, to glimpse its radiant smile and comprehend its peace."

A strange thing happened. Within a few minutes, the whole experience started to make complete sense to me. Reid had placed my solo climb of Peaks 11,200 and 11,286 correctly in the larger context, of my previous climbing experiences and of my entire life. All my life I had been looking into a hazy mirror, and after 31 years the fog had lifted. I could see myself, everything about myself, all crystal clear, all making perfect sense. I had nearly touched the inevitable on Table Mountain, had accepted my fate, and then lasted to see another sunset. This is what life was all about.

Solo. A performance by one person alone; without a companion or partner. In mountaineering, possibly the ultimate test of one's mental and physical capabilities. That was what made the religion of climbing so different. I didn't need a preacher to tell me what to think, to tell me what to feel, to interpret my own feelings and experiences. The wilderness was my church, the mountain my sermon; my gear, techniques, and knowledge my bible. What I only now understood was the true power of climbing.

You can lie to your friends, you can spin an exaggerated story, and if you're a good actor you might even be able to pull off a show in front of your climbing partners...but only a complete idiot lies to oneself. In soloing, be it rock climbing, mountaineering, hiking, or whatever, test your limits to the very edge, and find out who you really are. You're all by yourself. Just you and the mountain. Lie to yourself—or the mountain—and you may come face to face with the inevitable. Be honest and you just may discover the ultimate truth.

Two months later, I did climb Mount Whitney, and not alone. But looking back on and comparing the two experiences, I can't help but think that my five and a half hours on Table Mountain were an incredible test of my mental and physical capabilities. Quite simply, it was the ultimate mountaineering—or more, religious—experience. I would have to make a lot more time in my life for this.

The Power Bar of Doom

This story has not been previously published.

There we were, about six or seven miles up a wicked singletrack so steep and rutted that we spent more time carrying our bikes than riding them. As the angle began to lessen and the ruts disappeared, an unspeakable horror appeared: poison oak lining the trail.

We had never been so far up this trail before, and were never likely to do it again. So rather than immediately retreating, Mike and I decided to hike up the trail a mile or two, just to check it out. I was dehydrated and starving, so I grabbed my last water bottle and the only food I had—a chocolate Power Bar.

I immediately noticed something a little odd about the Power Bar—that the foil wrapper was worn down. Upon opening the forsaken beast, I then observed that the corners were sort of grayish. Oh, well. A little dirt never hurt a mountain biker. I wolfed down the Power Bar with joy. And being a good boy as well, I folded the wrapper up and stuck it in my pocket.

After about a mile and a half, we turned around and returned to our bikes. The ride down was quite interesting. At one point, riding down some nightmarish section singletrack I had been forced to walk up an hour earlier, I was descending at an almost imperceptible crawl when my front tire got stuck solid in a rut. It was the ultimate slow motion endo. As the back end of the bike slowly lifted, my weight shifted forward, and just as I was about to go over the handlebars, everything froze. With my body and bike perfectly balanced over the front tire, I was suspended in space long enough to turn back and say "Hey, Mike, check this out!" When I got bored with trying to maintain my balance, I gently shifted my weight back, jumped off, and walked the bike down the rest of the rough part.

Back at my house that afternoon, we were both pretty beat. In a semi-vegetative state, we watched "The Big Lebowski" and a couple other movies for five or six hours, then Mike had to go home and study for some frigging test for his MBA program.

I think it was about 11 p.m. when all hell broke loose. To quote the old Monty Python skit about some cheap Australian wine, "it really opened up the sluices at both ends." The kind of vomiting my friend Dave described best, where the blast is so powerful it's as if you're hanging on to the bowl for dear life, your legs flapping uselessly behind you in the shock wave, like a shredded flag in a tornado.

About four or five days after the fateful mountain biking trip, when I could think straight again, I sent Mike an email. We determined that the only thing we had eaten differently that say was the Power Bar I had. I dug the wrapper out of my pants pocket and discovered that the bar had expired long ago. And the holes worn in the corners of the wrapper took on an entirely new perspective after staring a toilet bowl in the face for untold hours, sweating out gallons of water while lying on the cold bathroom tile, wishing in vain I could just die. Complete recovery took several weeks.

The infamous wrapper is now nailed to the wall in my garage. On top is mounted a plastic Halloween skeleton. It's my monument to the Power Bar of Doom, a constant reminder to be careful what I eat.

Dawn Patrol
Imagine Joshua Tree National Park
All To Yourself...

This story was originally published in Issue #7 (July/August 1997) of mOthEr rOck magazine.

Thursday, May 15th. Why was my alarm going off at the ungodly hour of 4:15 a.m.? Oh, yeah, I was supposed to go bouldering on my way to work. But the three hours of sleep I got wasn't cutting it. I decided to do that fatal thing so many people do in this kind of situation: "I'll just close my eyes and rest for five more minutezzzzzz..."

Only a minute or two into it, my wife was seemingly screaming in my ear "Aren't you supposed to go climbing?" She wasn't yelling of course—she was actually asking very politely in a near whisper, but it sure shattered my peaceful state as well as any screaming could have. O.K., maybe I should actually get up and do this thing. Got to save face and all. Maybe I'll just go and scope out a few areas I've never seen before.

By 4:30 a.m., all the junk was in the car, including the essentials like a change of clothes, deodorant, my briefcase, and about 20 CDs. Oh, yeah, and climbing shoes, chalk bag, and tape.

It had all started about a year ago, in the summer of 1996, when Matt McGunigle and I needed a change to our

Tuesday/Thursday dawn workouts at Mt. Rubidoux. "Joshua Tree," I said, at first almost in jest. "It won't get too hot out there until about 8, 8:30. We could be in to work by 10, 11 at the latest." After I talked him into it, I managed to talk myself into it as well. We adopted the term "Dawn Patrol" for our insanity, and on one early morning session at Real Hidden Valley even coincidentally ran across some graffiti that said "Dawn Patrol" scrawled on a concrete picnic table. It was then sealed in stone. We weren't Stonemasters, we were Dawn Patrollers. We couldn't lead *Valhalla*, but we damn sure could get up at four o'clock in the morning to go climbing!

This time, though, I was by myself. It was getting increasingly difficult to find partners to join me in such an act of temporary insanity. They claimed their schedules were too busy. But I knew the truth: they thought I should be committed. Whatever. With the sun rising over the windmill-covered hills and the Beastie Boys screaming "So Whatcha Want?" inside the car at full volume, J-Tree autopilot easily guided me to my destination.

By 6 a.m., I was in the Hidden Valley parking lot, scoping a few of the boulders that didn't have campers snoring at the bases. *Caveman*, B2—a long, overhanging traverse on Huecos through a cave—was a lovely looking problem that reminded me of the lower (easier) half of *Latin Swing*, 5.11b, on the Solosby formation in Real Hidden Valley. There were a couple of good looking moderate climbs here as well, including *Split Grain*, a 5.8 arête, and *Bushwhack*, a 5.9+ lieback crack. There are lots of problems in this area, but it can be pretty limiting when the campsites are occupied, which is about 365 days a year. I bailed.

Off to Echo Cove, to check out the problems there. It was perfect. It was starting to warm up, and nobody was camping at the bases of the problems. I tried to warm up on the Arête Boulders, which are rated "5.9 to 5.10+; many problems" in Craig Fry's guide, but had no luck. (Later, back at the car, Mari Gingery's guide told me why: I had been attempting to warm up on a couple of 5.11b/c problems. Ooops. Was I sandbagged, or just stupid?). I then moved to the fabulous *Echo Cove Thin Crack*, a right-slanting 5.11b or so. On my third try, at the crux with both hands in the thinnest usable part of the crack, I moved my feet up and was ready to commit to the move up to the "good" hold higher up, after which it would supposedly get easier. Suddenly, one of my feet popped, and I landed poorly on a sharp rock, tweaking my right ankle. In pain, I immediately changed back in to walking shoes. Things didn't look good. That was probably it for the day, if not a couple of weeks.

If I could no longer climb, at least I could check out some of the other bouldering Joshua Tree had to offer. Next, off to the Peyote Cracks on the Baby Apes formation across from Echo Rock. What a disappointment. These cracks looked doable— 5.8 to 5.11a, with the cruxes down low—but they were horribly high, up to 30 or maybe 35 feet. Call me a wimp, but there was no way I would touch these without a toprope. By this time the throbbing pain in my ankle had almost completely subsided, so maybe it was time to check out something more to my liking.

I had never been to the Joshua Tree tourist trap known as Barker Dam, but nobody in their right mind would be there at this hour of the morning. So off to the Barker Dam trail I went,

25

to look for wildlife and try a few problems. Near the parking area, the Indian Wave boulder had an interesting problem to offer called *Old Wave*, 5.11a or b. Too bad I didn't have the energy to pull the first move. To the northeast was a boulder more to my liking. I flashed *Liquid Wrench*, 5.10d, a traverse up a large flake. On this same formation, *Chicken Wing* has to be one of the most interesting moderate boulder problems I've ever done. Have you ever done a 5.9 that gets you horizontal? The start is a huge pinch with the right hand and a small face hold with the left hand; the right foot is heel-hooked under, and the left foot dangling. From this position, you move up to a right-slanting crack on the face above. This climb was very strange, in a good way.

The dam itself was a bust. While I didn't expect Lake Michigan, what I saw was a 40 foot by 40 foot pool of muck, inhabited by two ducks and a million mosquitoes. And the worst part was that the big boulder protruding from the muck looked like it might have a good moderate problem or two on it.

On the second half of the loop, I swung by the Piano Boulder. *Piano Rock Crack*, 5.8/9, was a nice crack but pretty off-the-deck—maybe 25 feet up. On the other side of the trail, *The Tube*, 5.10d, looked like a nice slanting crack to a fairly sick mantel. I then walked over to the famous *Gunsmoke*, a classic long 5.11 traverse. Working on pieces for a while, I noticed how smooth all the holds were—this route obviously sees heavy traffic, and I can understand why. It's beautiful.

It was getting hot, and getting late. I quickly jogged back to the car, doused my head with water, used my smelly shirt as a towel, changed in to my work clothes, and dabbed on a little deodorant to mask at least part of the stink. It was 8:30 a.m.

Except for a quick pit stop at Del Taco in Yucca Valley for a breakfast of chicken soft tacos and a caffeine-blaster 32 ounce Diet Coke, it was a straight shot back to Redlands. I was in to work by 10:15 a.m., had no voicemail messages, only 41 e-mails messages, and nobody even seemed to miss me.

Another 200 miles on the car, and I had only done a few problems. But the morning had been an overwhelming success, taking me to a whole slew of new problems. Sitting at my desk, staring cross-eyed at the skin pealing from my hands and drinking my fifth Diet Coke in a futile attempt to stay awake, I couldn't help but think: isn't it wonderful to be a climber living in Southern California?

Confessions of a Dirtbag

This article originally appeared in issue #93 (05.15.2002) of Dirt Rag magazine.

It all started on the ski slopes of Southern California, but we weren't mountain biking. It was 1981, before mass acceptance of such mainstays as mountain bikes and snowboards, in the heyday of heavy metal and big hair. We were typical college students—post-high school, pre-career, looking for fun. So we took up skiing.

The hurdle we encountered was that we were poor. Lack of cash can be a substantial stumbling block in a money-intensive pastime like skiing. Even in 1981, the equipment was expensive, and skiing was rapidly becoming less a sport and more a Yuppie-fashion show statement.

Enter Mike, my good friend since grade school. People who don't know Mike often call him a cheap bastard. People who know him well agree, but openly only refer to him as "thrifty." He showed us how to break into the big scene with minimal investment: we cruised the thrift shops and, for a total outlay of less than $15, hacked together a crappy conglomerate of discarded and ex-rental skis, bindings, and boots.

Our equipment looked like crap compared to the then-state-of-the-art dream gear strapped to the feet of the Yuppies on the slopes, but it worked. And to distract everyone from the junk strapped to our feet, we Yuffies (self described "Young Urban Failures") made a bold, grassroots fashion statement by only skiing in T-shirts and blue jeans.

Sure, we were laughed at by the Yuppies and ridiculed by the ultra-hip, but we took the ultimate high road by being anti-hip and beyond cool, adopting a posture that is almost timeless in a world increasingly defined by fleeting fads and fashion.

In a few short years, our motley group of dirtbag skiers began to fall apart as we graduated from college, got good jobs, and gradually upgraded to "real" skis and garb. But skiing was never again as fun as the glory years of dirtbag skiing, and the expensive skis now sit in our garages, collecting dust and cobwebs.

My first exposure to mountain bikes came in 1985. Darrell Palmer and I were hiking the dirt road up to Mt. Baldy ski resort, and a dude edged past us on a strange machine that looked like a hybrid between a beach cruiser and a 10-speed. He explained it was called a "mountain bike," and I instantly wanted to try one.

This was back when mass-market "bikes" were cheap knock-offs of 10-speed road bikes; a "true" mountain bike was out of my price range. I set about taking the components off my old 10-speed, and mixing them with the frame and wheels on an old junked beach cruiser. Countless hours and $0 later, I had a huge pile of junk in the middle of the garage, and lots of pent-up frustrations. And still no mountain bike.

Enter the Murray. The concept of finding a cheap, under $200 mountain bike was revolutionary. It was 1987, and I finally experienced the thrill of mountain biking. Sure, it was only 10 speeds for pushing the 50-plus pound solid steel monster up the steep So Cal fire roads. But it was a mountain bike. And it was mine.

Adventures of the Mediocre
A Guided Ascent of Mt. Whitney's Mountaineer's Route

This story appeared in Issue #3 (November/December 1996) of mOthEr rOck magazine.

"The heroes I admired in my youth seemed to possess abilities and virtues beyond the grasp of ordinary men. My desire to emulate them was very great but never succeeded in approaching their high standards.

"I discovered that even the mediocre can have adventures and even the fearful can achieve."

—Edmund Hillary, *Nothing Venture, Nothing Win*, 1975

Edmund Hillary was my hero, and as can only be expected my attempts to emulate him fell far short of the high standards he set. My own visions of adventure started before I can remember, but in the late 1970s began to focus on something that seemed achievable, even if slightly mediocre. Like Hillary, I wanted to climb a mountain. Unlike Hillary, my mountain was not necessarily Mt. Everest.

My cousin Jeff had given me a copy of a booklet called *Climbing Mount Whitney* by Wheelock and Condon. For several years, together Jeff and I plotted our strategy for hiking the 11 mile trail to Whitney's summit. At 14,494 feet, the highest point in the continental United States, it was the crown jewel of the royal Sierra Nevada range, and a milestone in the life of many with interests in hiking or mountaineering. And with some 6,200 feet of elevation gain from the trailhead to the summit, this was no stroll in the park. It would be our adventure. Our mediocre Everest.

Over the next ten years, the dream slowly faded. Little things like college, career, and family seemed to put even more distance between Mt. Whitney and me. The final series of nails in the Mt. Whitney coffin were revelations of the severe overcrowding on the peak…a lottery system for permits to hike to the summit…tales of 200 people intimately sharing the summit on a holiday weekend…even a toilet on the summit. A true *un*wilderness experience. So I moved on to somewhat wilder, less traveled, and lower peaks.

Yet the dream of Mt. Whitney — *the tall one* — continued to gnaw at my spirit. More than a dozen years after my initial adolescent crush with Whitney, I decided to revisit the possibility of ascending this mountain. And with some four years of technical rock climbing experience, surely there must be another way to the summit. If I could not avoid the crowds at the destination, at least I could avoid the freeway leading there by taking a back road.

It turns out that the freeway, er, trail is not the only way to the top. A number of technical rock climbing routes lead up the

East Face of Mt. Whitney, by far the two most popular being the classic East Face Route (first climbed by Sierra mountaineering legends Norman Clyde, Jules Eichorn, Glen Dawson, and Robert Underhill in 1931), and the much more aesthetic East Buttress Route. Yet my most exciting discovery was something called the Mountaineer's Route.

On October 21, 1873, John Muir, father of the Sierra, summitted Mt. Whitney by a new route. Up until this time, the mountain had only been climbed by less technical routes, for the most part roughly following the route of today's popular hiking trail. But Muir ascended the mountain by way of the couloir between Whitney's East Buttress and North Face: the Mountaineer's Route. The first "technical" route up Mt. Whitney. My adventure had been identified.

Questioning my own mountaineering skills, and bowing to concerns from my family as to the safety of such an undertaking, I wondered if this route was something that I should even consider. A climb such as this must be worth the risk. At the same time, risk should be minimized to an acceptable level. How could I reduce the risk yet still have my adventure?

Mountain guides, immensely popular in areas such as the Alps, are somewhat a rarity in many parts of the United States. I was not too crazy about using guides, especially on something as "tame" as Mt. Whitney, until I read a paragraph in the book *Ascent* by Jeremy Bernstein, where he describes the death of his friend Georges. "I looked forward to seeing (Georges again)," says Bernstein, "but before we could meet he was killed. His death made a deep impression on me. Apart from anything else, it convinced me once again of the extreme dangers involved in climbing, even for climbers as skilled and experienced as Georges was. I decided that I myself would never climb anything really difficult without a guide." While a guide obviously cannot guarantee a climb completely without risk, surely tapping the vast experience of a guide increases your odds of having a safe trip. Bernstein convinced me that a guide was a reasonable precaution for those of us craving mountaineering but not yet ready to make the ultimate sacrifice for it.

The guide we chose, Todd Vogel, was a veteran of Sierra Nevada climbs. He had been to the summit of Mt. Whitney some seventeen times—by way of the Mountaineer's Route, the East Face Route, the East Buttress Route, and other routes. A man after my own heart, he had never been to the top of Whitney by way of the main hiking trail. And with him, we managed to feel much safer.

In the parking lot at Whitney Portal, we made the final preparations for our three days on Mt. Whitney. As it turned out, Jeff could not make the trip, but my old friend Steve had stepped in to join me. My pack had seemed surprisingly light, and it had been; only 30 pounds with empty water bottles and lacking the few minor pieces of group equipment to be supplied by our guide. Now at the trailhead, with my three quarts of water, group food, a stove, a rope, a climbing harness, and other miscellaneous supplies, a terrible thing had happened—my moderate pack had grown into a 60+ pound monster. Steve's pack was no better. It was going to be a long, long way to the top...

As it turns out, it was a long way just to the trailhead. We had parked in the "overflow parking" section at Whitney Portal, which meant a five minute hike up the main road to get to the trailhead. That short hike was a spirit-buster, and it was only the beginning. Just two or three minutes into the hike, I could think of only one thing: I was dead meat. Arriving at the "official" trailhead at exactly 11 a.m. Wednesday morning, we immediately started up the trail. It was wide, and gently graded for the most part. And I felt like I was dying. My back was already aching from the weight of my pack. How on earth could I make it?

After a short time on the trail, things got better as I found my rhythm. Soon we had arrived at a fork in the trail. To the left, the main hiking trail continued for 11 more miles to the summit. To the right, the Mountaineer's Route—to the same summit, with the same elevation gain, but covering less than half the mileage. It doesn't take a calculator to figure out the one word that best describes this route: steep.

Veering to the right, a dramatic change occurred almost instantly. Gone was the wide and gently graded trail. U.S. Forest Service trail engineers had spent a lot of time and thought on the design of the main trail. Mountaineers had designed our route by trudging upward with barely a glance at their feet. Eyes were on the lofty goal, the rocky point piercing the heavens, not the optimal foot placement. People didn't hike up this way to sightsee. If you were on this trail, you were *climbing* Mt. Whitney.

Our legs functioning like huge hydraulic pistons, we propelled ourselves and our packs of lead upwards towards the

Ebersbacher Ledges, the first semi-difficult section of the trip. Heading up Lone Pine Canyon we followed rough trails up both sides of the canyon until we arrive at a steep section of the canyon that looks impossible. While not actually impossible, there is a relatively easier way around this obstacle. We crossed to the north side of the creek and climbed the north wall of the canyon. Here a series of huge, near-vertical ledges act as switchbacks. These were the Ebersbacher Ledges I had been reading about. The exposure was invigorating, and only one spot—a couple of dicey moves while transitioning from one ledge up to a higher one—seemed really dangerous. "If we need to, we can take off our packs here and pass them up," said Todd. But we managed to surmount this test piece with our packs still riveted to our backs. After some more very breathtaking exposure, the ledges eventually dumped us out back in Lone Pine Canyon, above the obstacles.

Todd was pushing us at a terrific pace. With our late start on the trail, this pace was necessary. "It would be really nice to get to our high camp tonight," he kept saying. "It would make our summit attempt tomorrow so much easier." I was all for easier. I was determined to push through to the high camp that afternoon, or evening if it came to that.

I had read several descriptions of the first day on the route, and one word had stuck out: demoralizing. By the time we reached Lower Boy Scout Lake at about 1:30 in the afternoon, I could have fallen asleep for quite some time. I was sore, tired, and most of all mentally exhausted. Instead of sleeping, we ate, and ate, and ate. Then, just when we were getting comfortable, Todd reminded us that two-thirds of our journey for the day was still ahead of us. So off we went, headed for Upper Boy Scout Lake.

We quickly fell back into pace, with Todd leading, me second, and Steve in the rear. Todd's pace was amazingly efficient. My personal pace would have actually been much faster, at least for a while—but in the long run would have been slower because of my frequent rest stops. I was the sprinter, the fool doing the 50-yard dash, while Todd was the veteran of the mountain marathon. "The single most important thing you need to do when hiking is to find the right pace for yourself," Todd said. And as a guide, he was doing his best to find the right pace for *us*. It was incredible. I was right behind him the whole time, hiking at about 99% capacity, but I could follow him without resting for up to 30 minutes.

Above Lower Boy Scout Lake we followed the south side of Lone Pine Canyon, up several hundred feet over some scree to pass another waterfall, and emerged on top to cross the creek. Suddenly we were on huge, low-angled granite slabs that extended for at least half a mile up the now very wide canyon. The canyon walls to each side of us consisted of beautiful gray granite cliffs, with a number of lazy waterfalls trickling down their faces leaving dark stains that looked like running mascara. The slabs in the canyon bottom were covered with the multiple threads of Lone Pine Creek, making for interesting mixed hiking and scrambling. We hiked past the last few trees, up a steep rocky pitch, and emerged at an amazing natural amphitheater framing Upper Boy Scout Lake.

We spent about an hour at the lake, snacking and soaking our tired feet in the near-freezing water. Todd pulled out a container of half-and-half and placed it in the cold water to chill. We watched trout jump after insects in the alpine lake. We admired the vertical rock face to the west, completely blocking our view of the East Face of Mt. Whitney that we knew was so close. A charter member of the Polar Bear Club, Todd took a brief swim in the frigid lake. And just as we were all getting really relaxed, it was time to go again.

The next 45 minutes or so consisted of a steep trudge up the southeastern wall of the lake, which put us at a plateau within striking distance of the summit. It was 5:30 p.m. Six and a half hours and 3,700 vertical feet after starting on the trail, we established base camp in a sandy, grassy meadow at an elevation of 12,000 feet, between Upper Boy Scout Lake and Iceberg Lake. The view of Mt. Whitney and the Sierra crest from this place could only be described as awe inspiring. From here, the great rock face of Mt. Whitney, standing just slightly higher than the adjacent spires of Keeler and Day Needles, simply took one's breath away. This was what we had come for. This was what mountaineering was all about.

Practically the only vegetation in this alpine desert was a few short, scraggly clumps of grass growing in peculiar rings. The rings were familiar; I had seen similar rings, but on a much larger scale, while doing research on Creosote bushes in the Mojave Desert. Creosote rings could reach a dozen or more yards in diameter, representing 10,000 or more years of plant cloning. But the rings of grass clones in this Sierra alpine desert measured only a few inches across. I had imagined the Mojave to be one of the most inhospitable places on Earth, but the six foot tall Creosote bushes made the Mojave look like a tropical rain forest when compared to the alpine desert of the Eastern Sierra.

Once camp was set up, Todd discovered he had made a terrible mistake: the half-and-half he had left in Upper Boy Scout Lake to chill was, well, still in the lake. Without a moment of hesitation, he decided to go back down for it. Donning sandals, he started running back down the slope that had almost killed us on the way up, shouting "time me" as he launched down the hill. Before too long, he was back, with the half-and-half in hand, still dripping a little from the extended chill in the lake. I checked the watch. His time: 22 minutes. "You've got to take a couple of minutes off that," Todd said. It seems that on his way back up he had stopped to chat with a couple of mountaineers. Oh, yes, and he had also taken the time for another quick dip in the lake. O.K., so we'll call it 20 minutes. Cardiovascular bastard.

After a relatively sleepless night at our base camp, we awoke the second morning in the dark at 4 a.m. Some oatmeal, some water (two quarts!), and a hit or two of espresso and the now-famous half-and-half, and we left camp by 5 a.m. Our headlamps traced a dim aura along the rough trail up from the campsite to Iceberg Lake. We passed another climbing party in the twilight, an eerie encounter between strangers who were by definition close friends. No words were necessary. We were kindred souls, of like mind and with similar goals. We were all obsessed with this mountain, and with a fair bit of luck we would all be on top in a short while.

We reached Iceberg Lake at an elevation of 12,500 feet shortly before 6 a.m. I drank another quart of water while watching the most magnificent sunrise on the Whitney massif. It was a tremendous sight as the sun peaked above the White Mountains on the opposite side of the Owens Valley, and illuminated the Sierra Crest in a rapidly changing palette of pinks and oranges. As the light show faded, we filled our packs with two more quarts of water from Iceberg Lake, donned our helmets, and hit the road. From this point on, the intensity would only keep increasing.

The Mountaineer's Route contained a large tongue of frozen snow, so we scrambled up the rocky slope around it to the left. This direct approach saved a little time and avoided the obvious hazards of dealing with the ice. Within 30 or 40 minutes, we joined the couloir above this icy patch. Back in the Mountaineer's Route proper, we were doing much more scrambling than hiking. The route was steep, rugged, and rocky, with talus, scree, loose gravel, and sand covering steeply angled slabs. Why, in a few parts, there was even a faint trail...

Our immediate goal was "The Notch," a prominent feature at approximately the 14,000 foot level that marked the end of the couloir and gave us our first views of the other side of the Sierra—and also of the North Face of Mt. Whitney, our last obstacle before the summit.

In most years, even in July and August, several large icy snow tongues plummet down the North Face and force a somewhat difficult passage for the mountaineer. The previous winter having been especially dry in the Sierra, we were lucky to find very little ice in our path—so little that Todd determined it was unnecessary for us to put on our climbing harnesses and traverse the obstacles as a roped team. We simply dropped down about 50 feet on the other side of The Notch and started traversing. After a few hundred yards and only two or three precarious foot placements, we turned upward towards the summit plateau. All that stood in our way was a few hundred feet of moderate Class 3 rock climbing. It was at times such as this that having a guide really paid off—in the jumble of thousands of ways to scramble up the mountain, Todd was able to quickly point us to the best route.

Once off the Class 3 rock and out on the summit plateau, we cached some of our gear and walked up the relatively gentle slope for a hundred yards or so. To our amazement, we summited at 9:25 a.m.—less than four and a half hours after leaving camp. We had gained 6,200 feet in elevation in less than 24 hours. I had broken my personal altitude record by a whopping 3,200 feet. And I felt great!

To our delight, there was only one other person on the summit—a rugged giant of a man from Colorado who had made the ascent by the popular hiking trail, from parking lot to summit in only five hours! His whole purpose for climbing the peak seemed to be to find a captive audience to air his complaints ("the trail was so boring," and "too many switchbacks!"). His displeasure with his ascent could not dampen my pleasure. I had gained my summit, and there were no crowds. The Mountaineer's Route had lived up to its promise as the back road to paradise.

The view from the summit and the plateau was so spectacular that it was mind numbing. An amazing side view of Keeler Needle...Mt. Russell and the gorgeous Fishhook Arête...the eastern half of Sequoia National Park...the Owens Valley and the White Mountains beyond...it was all just too much to take in.

"Remember," Todd had reminded us on the way up, "the summit is only 49% of the climb. You still have to get back down." Clouds were building to the southwest, and the weather forecast called for rain. Leaving the summit at about 10:45 a.m., we hurriedly retraced our steps back to our cache of gear. Rather than heading straight down the North Face from our cache, we continued west for another few hundred yards. This tactic enabled us to avoid most of the Class 3 down climbing, and just added a little to the length of our traverse back to The Notch.

We continued our cloud watch through the rest of the descent, as the white puffs became more frequent and eventually started to block the sun. But to our enjoyment, it didn't rain. Even with the thought of being trapped in a sudden downpour always in the backs of our minds, we were able to enjoy the incredible views on the decent. Victory was sweet.

Back in camp by 1:30 p.m., we quickly began the recovery process. We ate, napped, and drank as much liquid as we could hold. And there was plenty of time to reflect upon the accomplishment of the day.

"The most enjoyable part of mountaineering is getting there," Todd had told us earlier. "The summit is a bonus." How true! The Mountaineer's Route was highly varied, and completely different from what I had imagined—a veritable treasure of mountaineering delights. The summit, however, was exactly as average as I had expected it to be—and maybe even somewhat of a disappointment. A great, rocky, gently sloping plateau. A toilet. A tin roofed building. The route up and down had been a summary of everything good about mountaineering. The summit became little more than a tick mark in my climbing diary.

That evening, we went to sleep early—well before dark. Soon the wind picked up, whipping violently between the sand and our floorless tent. Why, Steve even tells me that at one point the tent collapsed on us, but I was too busy sleeping...

Friday morning. It was time to go home, to leave our miniature adventure and return to our regular lives. Leaving camp and our million dollar view of Mt. Whitney and the Sierra Crest behind, it was time to return to the rat race that we had worked so hard to escape. Yet ironically it was this same rat race that had provided the money, the gear, and the guide that made the trip possible. It was the viscous circle of the part-time mountaineer.

It could have been the air getting increasingly thicker with every downhill step, or possibly the continued exhilaration of having made the summit, or maybe we were just in better shape...whatever the reason, our 60 pound packs suddenly felt as light as feathers.

Reversing the course that so recently we had toiled over, we raced down the mountain. Before long, our bleak alpine desert was behind us and we were again surrounded by a few trees, then quickly by a forest of green. Pausing to look back at Mt. Whitney whenever we could, we were reluctant to say good-bye to our new friend.

"We are now leaving civilization," said Todd, "and entering chaos." Twenty feet later, we dropped off the steep trail of the Mountaineer's Route and rejoined the main Mt. Whitney trail. Within 30 seconds we were treated to the sights of countless tourists and day trippers, many clearly unprepared for even the shortest day hike in an environment such as this. More people passed us in the first three minutes on the trail than we had seen on the Mountaineer's Route in the last three days. There was even trash on the trail. Hearts sank as the mediocre mountaineers realized that the adventure was truly over. Fond memories and fading photographs would have to sustain our desires for adventure, until the next time.

In the modern classic *Mountains of the Great Blue Dream*, Robert Leonard Reid best sums up the credo of the mountaineer.

> "Mountain climbers positively relish the almost perfect rigor of their discipline's cardinal directive: Go to the edge and perform flawlessly, and you will survive (probably) to go to the edge again. How delicious!"

That evening, savoring soup and burritos back at camp, was a time for reflection.

"So," Todd asked, "was it harder or easier than you thought it would be?"

"Harder," Steve said quickly. "Harder."

"It was exactly like I thought it would be," I replied without even thinking. "I thought it was going to kick my ass, and that's exactly what it did."

We had climbed and returned from our mediocre Everest, and would undoubtedly be back in years to come to conquer many others. We were hooked. *Viva la mediocre!*

Muddy Little Secret

This story ran in Issue #1 (Summer 1999) of FunPig magazine.

It's January, and I'm sick of my job. Smack in the middle of trying to play catch-up from the extended holiday season when nothing much gets done, throw in planning for the new year, numerous budgets, and annual employee reviews. It's insane.

As if that's not bad enough, January is often the month when you really notice the weather start to turn in Southern California. Our four to five weeks of so-called "winter" had come at the worst possible time for me, making outdoor stress relief activities a hit-or-miss proposition.

It's a Tuesday afternoon, almost 2 p.m., and I'm feeling the itch. Having just turned in the last of the damned plans, budgets, and reviews, I was free. The only hurdle left to overcome was the fact that it was raining like hell. It had been all day.

But wait—was that a brief flicker of sunshine through the window? It was! A quick glance at the LA radar site on the Web (remind me, how the heck did we live our lives before the Internet?) revealed a break of maybe a couple of hours between two big storm fronts. The first one had just passed, having soaked the hillsides behind my house, and brought the snow level down to 3,500 feet in the San Bernardino Mountains. The second front promised even colder temperatures, even more moisture, and a snow level predicted in the 2,000 foot range, which would put it right about level with the top of my chimney. The window of opportunity was brief, and narrowing further with every minute as the front quickly moved eastward.

I felt sneaky, almost guilty as I ditched out the back door and headed to my car. Already having a somewhat questionable reputation at work—"Hey, it's 2:45, what are you still doing here? Ha ha ha..."—I had nothing to lose. I rationalized that I was just living down to their expectations.

Twelve minutes later I pulled into my driveway, and the hills of East Highlands Ranch looked breathtaking. To the west, the clouds were closing in. And I surmised the trails must be pretty muddy.

The choice seemed obvious—The Serpent, one of my favorite trails. At a little under three miles and starting two minutes from my door, it was far from epic; but under the circumstances, I'd take whatever I could squeeze in. I'd get one lap for sure, then depending on the conditions, maybe get lucky and go back for more. Virtually my own private trail, it consisted of less than a mile of rough pavement, a mile on dirt roads through orange groves, and a beautiful one mile section of singletrack. The singletrack consisted of a good climb at the beginning, with only one other (minor) climb towards the middle. The rest was flat to slightly downhill, coiling like a snake in and out of small drainages along the south side of the foothills. Like most singletrack in the area, it was mostly well graded, following an old dirt road that had been overgrown for many years.

As I began carving my way up the trail, the only other tracks were those from a coyote. While other mountain bikes were a fairly rare sight up here, their tracks usually lasted a while. Today, the rain had obliterated all of that and more. It was just me and the coyote. He was just doing his job, looking for dinner; I was ditching my job, looking for fun in the mud.

I soon realized that of the countless times I had ridden this trail, this was my first time in the mud. My pace was significantly slower, but that didn't matter, as the trail took on an entirely different character. To my right, the damp brush glistened with a fresh intensity, and barely 1,000 feet above me, the snowline brilliantly framed the picture. To my left, a magnificent sight developed as the sky darkened, the clouds rolled closer, and one small patch of sunlight illuminated the wet runway at San Bernardino International Airport.

Huge bands of rain could be seen to the west, and then to the south in Loma Linda. Weaving around mud puddles in front of me, I was comfortable in my familiar surroundings yet invigorated by this new interpretation of an old classic. It even smelled different. But all too soon, it was over. The rapidly approaching storm ruled out a second lap on The Serpent. I pointed La Machine back towards civilization.

As I entered my nice warm house and poured myself a bowl of hot soup, I wondered if the coyote ever caught his vermin for his own dinner. The fresh minestrone in my bowl blended perfectly with the smell of wet sage and other native aromatic herbs that still permeated my clothing from the ride. Then, as I finished the last spoonful of soup, I heard it. Pounding the sides of the house with a wind-driven vengeance, the rain was back.

My tire tracks would be erased within a matter of minutes, as would the tracks left by my comrade the coyote. Like it never even happened. Nobody else would ever know. It would be our little secret.

Ultimate Air
Mountain Biking and the Hutchinson Effect

This article was originally submitted to <u>Dirt Rag</u> *in December 2000, but it was never published.*

As I whip around another turn on my favorite singletrack, I contemplate the dawn of this new century. What monumental changes will the next 100 years bring? And who are the people walking among us who will make those changes possible?

Once every few hundred years, a person comes along who changes the world in a most astounding way—a revolutionary genius. Amongst the fleeting famous and the evolutionary geniuses, the revolutionary geniuses are typically not fully recognized during their lifetimes, their ideas being so radical, so mind boggling, that they cannot be fully realized, capitalized upon, or even comprehended by their contemporaries. The mad scientists and loose cannons of today just might be the heroes of tomorrow.

Copernicus was censored for thinking outside of the box, yet years later, all but a few freaks agree the world isn't the center of the universe. Socrates knew what he was on to, but most of his contemporaries just didn't get it—and he died for it. Not even Guttenberg could have comprehended the proliferation of books, magazines, newspapers, and other printed materials that today put the "mass" in mass media. And at some point in the future, when cars hover effortlessly above the pavement in Blade Runner fashion and space travel becomes as inexpensive as making a long distance phone call, John Hutchinson just may be recognized as the man who made it all possible.

In 1979, John Hutchinson was making history in his cramped living quarters in Vancouver, Canada. More of a scientific tinkerer than a formal scientist, Hutchinson surrounded himself with numerous pieces of surplus electronic equipment salvaged from Canadian naval vessels and other sources. By linking these disparate pieces of equipment together in ever more intricate patterns, he stumbled upon a single solution to two phenomena previously though possible only in exotic and unbelievable science fiction thrillers: levitation, and fusion of dissimilar materials.

Small objects began to hover. Then heavier objects began to hover. Then the objects began to accelerate. When it was over, solid pieces of metal had changed structure, and wood had merged at the molecular level with steel.

Levitation. Think of the possibilities for the future. When fossil fuels are exhausted, the cars and rockets of the future are propelled by the Hutchison Effect. Anti-gravity becomes commonplace, as we say goodbye to the technological curse of the twentieth century—the inefficient, polluting, noisy combustion engine.

I come off the singletrack, and decide to take the long way back. Looping dirt roads and trails through the orange groves lead me all too quickly back towards home. Looking for one last thrill before the drudgery of the work day begins, I aim the bike towards the six foot BMX jump next to the road. It's the cherry on top of the sundae.

Down the hill, gaining speed. Up the ramp. For a brief moment, I become weightless. My body fuses to my bike; skin and bone become one with metal and rubber. The me-bike levitates, hovering in mid-air above the hard-packed dirt. Then, all too quickly, we slam back to Earth—and reality. Like the inanimate objects in a Hutchinson experiment, the otherworldly experience lasts for only a moment or two —but that moment or two can have a profound impact on one's existence.

Although the levitation is over almost immediately, my soul remains fused with the bike. The Hutchinson effect lives. I experience it for a brief moment almost every day, on a non-descript patch of dirt in the hills of Southern California.

Some day, maybe in 50 years, maybe in 100, the world could very well be a very different place because the discoveries of John Hutchinson might make the stuff of science fiction a reality. Until then, only a select few people can experience the levitation and fusion of dissimilar materials known as Hutchinson Effect. So get on your mountain bike and fly.

The Adventures of Matt & Matt
The 24 Hour Grand Tour of the Eastern Sierra

This story was originally published in Issue #6 (November 1996) of What's the Beta?

Some people tend to do crazy things when they get married and start a family. Like sell the sports car and use the cash to buy a mini-van. Get to sleep before Letterman comes on. And spend more money buying stock than buying beer. Why, I've heard that some guys even have to cut back on climbing or give it up all together.

But those guys are fools. You *can* have your cake and eat it too; you just have to be a little more creative, a little more flexible. Wash lots of dishes, do a ton of laundry, maybe even mop the kitchen floor for her once in a while, and you might be able to pull off the occasional pity climbing trip for a couple of days every year or two. But sometimes, that's just not enough. You need a more frequent fix.

There is a solution.

Enter the concept of the 24-hour Eastern Sierra road trip, or as we like to call it, The Adventures of Matt & Matt. The idea is simple: 24 hours is not a long time to be away from the wife and kids, since you usually work 10 hours a given day they'd probably be sleeping for another 12 of those hours. So you're really only impacting them by about 2 hours. Don't try to figure this out. That's our logic, and we're sticking to it.

The three basic rules of the road trip are simple.

1. Drive to and from your destination in the dark as much as possible.
2. Climb while it's light.
3. You can sleep a bunch when you get back home.

Read them, read them again until committed to memory, finish reading this article, and then eat this piece of paper.

I picked up Matt McGunigle (another Matt with a wife and two young children; I pick my partners according to very strict criteria) at his house in Riverside, and at 7 p.m. we hit the road blazing north towards Highway 395. We had three pounds of snack foods, three gallons of water, about 30 CDs, and a single purpose: to get to The Buttermilks by midnight. The sun quickly faded as we powered the Mother Rock Mobile up the 395 through the bowels of the Southern California desert. Driving straight through, we were in Bishop by a respectable 11 p.m. A quick stop at Giggle Springs gas station and mini-market (a mandatory stop when driving through Bishop; giggling is optional, but strongly encouraged) supplied us with the three forms of fuel we needed: a full tank of gas, a couple of 22 ouncers, and of course some more fatty snack foods. We hit the road again as quickly as possible, and were in the dirt parking lot at The Buttermilks a little after 11:30 p.m.

The Peabody Boulders, more commonly referred to as The Buttermilks, constitute a world-class bouldering area located about ten miles west of Bishop. My only other trip there had ended in disaster, when it started snowing as soon as we had stepped out of the car. I was weak, the rock was wet, and the only thing that didn't completely suck that day was running in to climbing bad boy Scott Franklin and talking to him for 15 minutes (he actually turned out to be one helluva nice guy!). Now, a year later, I was back, and intended to really get to know the place. We threw our bags down underneath the Birthday Boulders on prime hardman real estate, popped our brews, and enjoyed Mother Natures' light show until we nodded off to sleep.

Itching to get started, I awoke about 4 a.m. to watch Venus rise over Buttermilk Dome. By 5:20 a.m. I was running around like a kid in a toy store, scoping out the routes, and taking pictures of the magnificent sunrise on the Sierra Crest. Matt woke up shortly after, and we had donned shoes and were on the rocks by 5:50 a.m.

First stop for us lightweights was Ranger Rock, where we did the 5.9 crack on the northeast face, followed by the 5.10a face on the southwest side. Next, we moved on to the Tut Boulder, cranking through the 5.10a on the west face (just right of the 5.8 lieback).

At The Cornerstones, I did by best onsight to date: the short but reachy (for my 5 foot 10 1/2 inch frame anyway) face was rated 5.10c according to the old out-of-print Bartlett and Allen guide. Matt did it on his second try; not bad for someone who had only been climbing for less than a year. Off to the fabulous Green Wall Boulder, where we did the juggy 5.9 crack on the right side, and floundered on some of the steep 5.10/5.11 face problems. We then moved over to The Buttocks Boulder, where Matt and I both onsighted the 5.10c plates route on the northeast side. It seemed very simple and straightforward after all the campusing we had done in my garage.

It was time to go. We were not yet sickly pumped, but we were after all on a mission: to get in as much of the Eastern Sierra as we could in a day, and still be home in time to kiss the kids goodnight. Heading back to the car, we couldn't help but crank through the 5.10b problem on the north side of the Grovel Roof. After a quick dose of much-needed humility while attempting the 5.11a's on the Birthday Boulders, we packed up the car and evacuated to that Eastern Sierra climbing shrine, Wilson's Eastside Sporting Goods. It was 7:50 a.m. Amazing what you can accomplish when you're on a mission. A mission from Mother Rock.

So was a good two hours of bouldering in the Eastern Sierra worth the total drive time of about ten hours? Of course it was.

But wait; that's only the beginning of our story. Arriving at Wilson's, we were among the first to get the fabulous brand new guidebooks to the Eastern Sierra, written by Marty Lewis and John Moynier. Long live climbing in the Eastern Sierra! Collect all three!

With the new guidebooks firmly in hand and Soundgarden blasting at a pleasantly uncomfortable level from the CD

player, we aimed the car north and floored it. Destination:
Deadman's Summit.

After some interesting routefinding, resulting in a loss of
about 45 minutes of precious time and the near-loss of the
Mother Rock Mobile to a raging river at the bottom of the
wrong dirt road, we found Deadman's areas #II and #III. Very
interesting rock here, unlike any I had ever seen before (but
have since seen at other Eastern Sierra areas such as Tall Boys
and The Stumps). The problems are usually pretty high off the
deck and steep, composed of a strange polished volcanic
surface sporting frequent incut "letterbox" holds and one- and
two-finger pockets. Starting to feel a little worked from our
two hour session at The Buttermilks, and not in the mood to
fully commit to any of the typically off the deck problems, we
stayed and played for about an hour and a half. Our favorite
problem was a nice 5.10b crack at Deadman's area #II. The
crux was the last move, high off the deck, with another face a
few feet from your back to glance painfully off of as you
plummeted to the rock-hard landing below. Not willing to risk
the possibility of ending the trip prematurely and on such a
bad note, we backed off.

Pumped and seemingly all climbed out for the day, we wanted
to at least lay eyes on that third most famous Eastside
bouldering area, Bachar Boulders. In a nutshell, we got lost. I
won't bore you with all of the sordid details. Suffice it to say
that the dirt roads around there are a maze, and while we saw
a lot of interesting territory, John's pumpstation was not in the
cards that day. After about 45 minutes, running out of patience
and precious time, we both looked at each other and said only

one word: "Iris." Stuff like that happens when you're both named Matt. And when you're on a mission.

Back in the days before development of the Owens River Gorge turned that destination into the Wal-Mart of Eastside climbing, Iris Slab was the most popular climbing spot in the Eastern Sierra. Located in a tranquil setting above Iris Meadows in stunning Rock Creek Canyon, it's a large, polished slab up to about 85 to 90 feet high with ten routes on it. Seven of the ten routes are 5.4 to 5.8, and there is not a single route on the rock that is not of either good or excellent quality. Combine these factors with the stunningly beautiful setting and the 15 minute approach, and it's no wonder that this is still one of the single most popular Sierra rocks outside of Yosemite. It's also a very popular site with local guides teaching beginning climbing classes.

As we trudged up the slopes leading to Iris Slab, carrying gear for the first time on the entire trip, we wondered if our Buttermilks/Deadman's biathlon had left us with any energy to complete the full triathlon. We eventually set a toprope above *Walking on a Thin Line*, the 5.7 on the right hand side of the slab. Great climb! But we were getting tired. It was getting late. We had had enough. Time to head back to the world of wives and kids, bills and jobs.

At the car, we were both thankful for the great day. After a brief heart-pounding moment where I thought I had locked the keys in the car, we were ready to motor. We shortly began to realize how utterly worked we were, and how nothing but snackables had been holding us over for the entire day. We could think of only one thing: somewhere along Highway 395, we had noticed on the drive up, there was a gas station. Inside that gas station was a Burger King. Inside that Burger King was an unlimited supply of 99 cent Whoppers. Soon, those Whoppers would be pulsating through our fat-clogged arteries. Let's ride!

Unfortunately, we had not remembered the exact location of the life-giving fast food joint. As it turns out, the Whopperdome was in Pearsonville, better known as The Hubcap Capitol of the World, and a good three hour drive from our last climb at Iris Slab. By the time we had reached the altar of saturated fat, our stomachs were speaking to each other in tongues. There was only one cure for such a supernatural exchange: two Whoppers each. With cheese!

We ate, we drove some more, and soon after dark we were home with our families. Was it worth it? By all accounts, yes. The Eastern Sierra is a huge buffet of countless classic lines and boulder problems. We hadn't stayed for the full seven course meal, but we had tasted a sampling of the appetizers. And it was good.

Death Valley ... By Kayak?

A different version of this story was originally published in the March 3rd, 2005 edition of the Highland Community News.

During the Ice Age, Lake Manly stretched more than 120 miles long and 20 miles wide across what we now call Death Valley. Today, this former lake is mostly a dry salt pan, known as the home of Badwater (at 282 feet below sea level, the lowest point in the western hemisphere). But thanks to El Nino and the record rainfall we experienced during the winter of 2004/2005, Lake Manly was back! After seeing a photo of two people kayaking Lake Manly, I tried for several weeks to get someone interested in making the trip. My old friend Mike finally agreed, and we left my house at 4 a.m.

By 8 a.m., we were scoping out the shoreline, trying to locate the best place to unload the kayaks. We settled on a spot about a quarter mile south of the Badwater parking area, and only had to carry the kayaks less than 100 yards to the water. We had heard that the lake was very shallow, and that we may have to walk the kayaks out quite a way until it was deep enough to float. But after walking less than ten feet through the water we realized it was already deep enough! It was a totally surreal experience, seeing this four by five mile lake where there wasn't supposed to be more than a few shallow pools of water, framed by stereotypical Death Valley geologic features to the east and the snow-covered Panamint Mountains to the west.

The first thing we did was paddle straight for the weather station, which was now partially under water of course. Next we paddled out to where we thought the lowest point in the western hemisphere was. We got very close, but without a GPS, we'll never know exactly. It was very strange, being a mile or two from shore, and dipping your paddle in and realizing the water was only about two feet deep. Mike thought since it was so shallow, maybe we could actually follow the hiking trail out to the lowest point—but the water was pretty murky, with a greenish-brown tinge to it. It seemed at least as salty as the ocean, but not nearly as salty as Mono Lake. The experience left a nice salt crust on everything—the kayaks, our legs, our clothes, even my camera.

When the wind turned the water from glass to ripples, and two more kayakers showed up and we no longer had the entire lake all to ourselves (yes, we're spoiled), we decided to move on. Our original plan was to check out the Amargosa River—a usually dry river that people had recently been kayaking down for 10 to 15 miles. But there just wasn't quite enough water in the river to do it easily. So on a whim, we headed over the Panamint Mountains and the White Mountains, over to Owens Valley to see if there was enough water in Owens Lake to kayak.

100 years ago, Owens Lake was large enough that paddlewheel boats regularly crossed its surface carrying mining supplies and silver, but that was before the City of Los Angeles bought up most of the land in Owens Valley and diverted the water south for urban use. After lunch in Lone Pine (where unfortunately clouds were obscuring the usually-

spectacular view of Mt. Whitney), we drove down to the lake. Sure enough, there was more water in Owens Lake than either of us had ever seen. But not wanting to carry the kayaks a mile or two from the car to the edge of the water, we spent more than an hour driving dirt roads trying to find an easy access point before calling it a day.

After 650 miles in about 14 hours, we were back at my house. Was it worth all that just for two hours of kayaking on a huge rain puddle in the middle of the Mojave Desert?

HELL YEAH!

Not Fixing Your Own Flats
...and the Decline of Western Civilization

This article originally appeared in issue #92 (May 2002) of Dirt Rag magazine.

It's my evening ritual; my therapy. While my kids bike, rollerblade, skateboard, and otherwise wreak havoc in the front yard, I pull up a lawn chair, pop open a cold beer, and pick the thorns out of my bike tires. Like monkeys picking the lice from each other, it's rooted in necessity, but has taken on a much deeper, therapeutic quality.

An interesting thing usually happens while stepping through this evening ritual. Right around the time I pop open my second beer, a steady stream of neighborhood kids walk up and ask me to fix their bikes. About 75 percent of these cases involve simple flat tires. Feeling a little loose from the liquor, and looking for cheap entertainment, I'll typically prod them for details, although the responses are sadly predictable: "My mom/dad won't be able to take it to the bike shop until Saturday..."

Bike shop? Excuse me? I may be willing to overlook the fact that most of these kids are old enough to be fixing their own flats. But why can't the parents fix them? Just like my dad did when I was a little kid, until I was old enough to get high sniffing the rubber cement on my own.

One particularly plentiful evening I was performing my ritual, and lost count at around 70 thorns between the front and back tires. Plink, plink went the thorns on the garage floor. It was a foregone conclusion that each tire would sport at least one hole. I was already prepared to patch the tubes, even before verifying a single puncture. And then I had a revelation.

You can partially blame the bike shops. They sell lazy Yuppie parents on the "free flat fixes forever" packages, both as an excuse to jack up the price of a mediocre bike, and as a ploy to get you back in the shop on a regular basis in order to talk you in to countless unnecessary "upgrades." But there's more to it than just that.

You can partially blame the kids. Most kids today are raised lazy. Hungry? Drive through Burger King. Flat tire? Drive through the bike shop. In addition, the whole concept of the flat is foreign to them. After all, they never get flats while riding BMX in 3Xtreme on Sony PlayStation.

The parents are to blame as well. If the family is lucky enough to have both parents living under the same roof these days, they probably both have to work just to make ends meet. When they get off work, there's barely enough time to shuttle the kids between soccer practice and piano lessons before ordering a pizza, rushing through homework, and passing out in bed, only to start the same vicious cycle all over again in a few short hours.

Maybe the real problem is more general. People in modern society are in a hurry. They're also dead lazy. They're too busy looking for quick, easy fixes to the ills of society to worry about locating and repairing a minuscule hole in a cheap piece of rubber. Just let the dude at the bike shop replace it. Surely it will leave more time in the day to worry about more important things.

Then again, it takes me about 20 minutes to drive to the bike shop and back, but I can fix a tire in three minutes flat.

The Ultimate Eastern Sierra Road Trip

This story first appeared in Issue #3 (November/December 1996) of mOthEr rOck magazine.

It was a perfect late summer day in the Eastern Sierra. A little hot in the sun, but perfect in the shade, with a nice breeze providing a fresh, cool feeling that reveals man's attempt at air conditioning for what it truly is: a dismal failure, a poor representation of perfection.

The pleasant roar of Rock Creek soothes my ears. The sharp smoothness of the grass in Iris Meadows caresses my toes. The incense of cedar and sage fills my nostrils. My senses combine to whisper one word to me over and over: "relax." This is quiet, peaceful time. Away from the distractions, annoyances, and petty problems of the so-called civilized world. Relaxing outdoors, over-stimulated by the simultaneous complexity and simplicity of nature, in a state that seems almost timeless, I listen to my senses and for a moment in time I merely exist.

But one of my senses is rebelling: my sense of sight. For across the meadow, on the other side of the river, beyond the pines, the cedars, the quaking aspens, and up the steep sage-covered slopes, lies a rock. It meshes perfectly with the surrounding environment, yet this integral component of the Sierra landscape has assumed a bloated status in my warped mind.

For I am a climber, and try as I may to listen to my brain and relax, some things are just not possible. And this is one of those times.

Towering above me and the meadow and the creek is the face of Iris Slab, one of the most popular climbing areas in the Eastern Sierra. It is calling me. Resistance is futile. I must climb it. After all, I wasn't here to relax. I was in the middle of a climbing safari of the Eastern Sierra. No time to power lounge in a meadow for three hours. Matt McGunigle and I were on a mission to climb like crazed lunatics for five days.

We eventually tear ourselves away from the comfort of our idyllic surroundings, and head up the "trail" to the base of the slab. Setting a toprope above *Welcome to the Iris Slab*, 5.8 ***, we find the right side of the slab tests the limits of doubling a 165-foot rope. Matt cruises the route, hesitating for only a second at the crux. But then, he's a good slab climber. Reluctantly, I step up to the rope next. I take my sweet time, finding two more cruxes than Matt did, but enjoying the climb quite a bit. It's definitely one of the better climbs on Iris Slab.

Next, using the same toprope, Matt heads up *Sting*, 5.8 **. He takes it a little slower this time, but still moves fluidly up the rock. Near the top, where the crack disappears, he pauses for a long time. He eventually places hand and feet tenuously on near-nothing holds, and gingerly powers his way over the top.

My ascent of *Sting* goes quite differently. When I get to the spot that stumped him, I pause for an eternity. Surely this cannot be 5.8!? My left foot begins to fall asleep due to a combination of boredom and still-not-yet-fully-broken-in Five.Ten Moccasyms.

When it's finally time to move that foot, I move it to a good hold, but my brain refuses to cooperate because of the lack of data flowing to it from the sleeping foot. I eventually pull off a sick, insane 5.10a traverse on nothing but dime edges and 75 feet of air, and finish off using the last 10 or 15 feet of *Welcome to the Iris Slab*, which seemed invitingly familiar the second time around.

Maybe after doing a multitude of 5.10 boulder problems the day before, I needed a dose of reality. Or maybe it's just the well-known fact that I suck at slab climbing. Whether it's making me cringe for mama on a 5.7, or spitting me off a 5.8 with glee, Iris Slab continuously humbles me. It teaches me that I still have much to learn in order to climb slabs well.

The day before had been very different, a definite feel-good day in every way. We awoke at The Buttermilks when the sun was warm, and decided to concentrate on the area around Grandma and Grandpa Peabody, the two largest boulders. We warmed up on the 5.9 on Baby Peabody, then moved over to the short, near-holdless (and—cringe—sort of slabby!) 5.10a on the boulder between Baby Peabody and Grandpa Peabody. We cooled down for a minute by doing one of the 5.8 (easy, but fairly exposed) routes on the left side of the main face of Sunshine Boulder. Then we worked the 5.10a/b route on the far right of the same face—I made it very high, with the last move clearly in reach, but just couldn't commit to such an off-the-deck problem so early in the trip. I ended up downclimbing it. Next time, toprope! (Yes, there is a nice shiny bolt on top right above the problem).

Moving on, we arrived at what must be my favorite rock at The Buttermilks—the Green Wall Boulder. After two years of attempting it and painfully stretching my finger tendons to the point of nearly snapping, this time I finally had the finger strength to crank the 5.10b on the left side. With that old monkey off my back, I followed with an onsight of the 5.10b route just right of the arête. Then, for the next half hour, I put in 12 to 15 tries on the 5.10c route left of center. Matt watched and rested through most of these attempts, pulling it off on his third or fourth try, while I fell from very high on my last try, my arms totally pumped from the many repeats. Oh, well, with the beta and fresh arms, I'll nail it next time on my first try. Something to look forward to—or obsess about—for the next trip.

Off to Wilson's Eastside Sporting Goods in Bishop. I needed tape if I was going to continue to climb for the entire trip. Besides, I'd been meaning to pick up a copy of John Sherman's bouldering bible *Stone Crusade*, and I knew Wilson's had it in stock. It made for great reading material for a road trip.

Our next destination was Deadman's Summit, the second world-class bouldering stop we'd make that day. Isn't climbing in California the greatest? Anyway, Matt and I had attempted a wonderful 5.10b finger crack at Deadman's two months prior, but had turned back near the top because it was so off-the-deck with an uncharacteristic (for Deadman's) very hard landing. We had vowed to return and toprope it.

Finding the route again was simple, while setting the toprope proved to be an arduous task. When we eventually got it set, the climb suddenly took on a ridiculous perspective. It looked very short, and it turned out to be just that. With the safety of a toprope, we had each topped out before we could even take a breath. It was somewhat of an anticlimax, after two months of obsessing over that crack; but it did feel good to finally do it. And hats off to Bachar and the other hard boys who must certainly have very large cajones to free solo routes much harder—and higher—than this one.

Using the same toprope (after an hour of setup and 30 seconds of climbing, I'll be damned if I was going to break it down just yet!), we moved right to a 5.10a face. I pulled it off, but was on the verge of coming off this vertical pocketfest almost the entire way. It seemed infinitely harder than the 5.10b finger crack we had just cruised! Next, Matt attacked the face, doing it with only one hang as he got three fingers painfully stuck in a two-finger pocket. Was that route really 5.10a? Looking at the topo later, I think we were off route and finished on the 5.10d face next to it. Or maybe Bachar is so damn good, he has no clue how to differentiate between 5.10a and 5.10d.

So my afternoon of slab sucking at Iris had been preceded by a wonderful day of bouldering at two of the premier bouldering spots in California, if not the entire U.S. I must try to conquer my slab hang-up. Pondering analytically, my poor slab performance was probably 10% sloppy footwork and 90% mental failure. I would work on my slab technique more in the morning, trying Iris Slab again. Matt had some ridiculous idea that we would try to toprope a 5.10a and a 5.10c—on a slab! But all I could think about was warming myself by the fire and popping a nice beer.

The next morning, we awoke cold and tired to watch the sunrise creep down the crest towards Iris Slab. Christian, Bob, and Joice had joined us in the night for brew and burritos. The five of us were now eating coffee cake and waiting for the sun to hit us, giving us a blast of warmth and a hint that climbing may in fact be possible on what seemed to be such a cold day.

The sun broke, and off we were to the slab—me with quite a bit of trepidation, with my unnatural fear of slabs haunting my every step. Under pressure from Matt, we jumped straight on my worst slabby nightmare—a toprope attempt of *Easy Way Out*, at 5.10a ** by far the most hideous slab route I had ever attempted, and about four grades beyond my slab comfort level. To my tremendous surprise, I cranked it without a single hang, never even getting out of breath or breaking pace. It actually seemed fairly easy. Hallelujah! My losing streak on slabs had been broken!

Feeling unstoppable, we upped the ante by two chips and moved to a toprope attempt of *Crazy Bald Head*, 5.10c ***. At the "bald" section the climb is named for, about two-thirds of the way up the route, I gave it a great try. Smearing and palming my way up the 20-foot blank section where dime edges were the jugs, I actually pulled off three consecutive moves on absolutely nothing before I had to hang. Matt and I both moved right towards the aptly named *Easy Way Out* to get around the crux, then finished off straight up—but not before pulling off some great 5.10b/c face moves. Although we had taken a slight detour, in general we were elated with our significant improvement in slab climbing for the day. It was hard to be at all disappointed with our performance! We finished out the morning with Bob, Joice, and Christian having

a great time toproping a series of climbs ranging from
5.4 to 5.7.

We quickly packed up our campsite in Iris Meadows to beat
the 2 p.m. "check-out time," and were heading south to Big
Springs campground...but not before a brief stop in Mammoth
for essentials (hot dogs, chili, ice, beer, and Carl's Junior).

Big Springs has got to be among the best campsites in the
Mammoth area, especially for climbers—it's free, in a beautiful
forested setting along the headwaters of the Owens River, and
within quick striking distance of Clark Canyon, Alpers
Canyon, The Stumps, Tall Boys, Rick's Rocks, and many other
climbing destinations including Deadman's Summit. After
reclaiming our primo campsite at Big Springs that we had
"reserved" a few days prior by leaving an ugly blue tarp and a
few empty water jugs, we were off on the dirt roads heading
north towards Tall Boys.

Five miles on mostly excellent quality dirt roads delivered us
to the "Indiana Summit Natural Area" sign where the
guidebook directed us to park for the short hike to Tall Boys. A
few hundred yards down the trail, we noticed a rocky outcrop
on our left. We followed this, and shortly the rock got to be
about 15 feet tall and overhanging. I saw some chalk on a few
holds. This must be it!

Tall Boys is the lesser known, less evil twin of Deadman's
Summit. Same type of rock, same letterbox slots. What Tall
Boys has over Deadman's is a much more pleasant, forested
setting; an almost complete lack of foot traffic; more usable
slots per square foot on the rock; and numerous climbs that are

less severe. At Deadman's, however, the rock is more highly polished, and more exposed to the sun, with an almost complete lack of the lichen that forms a vertical carpet of black velvet on many of the problems at Tall Boys.

We worked the excellent 15-foot tall overhanging boulder several times, doing a nasty face full of dynamic moves, then an odd but somewhat easier arête where I had to throw my left foot around the edge in sort of a side-pull heelhook for balance. We then continued south along the outcrop, doing a series of increasingly higher and higher (and mostly easier) slab and vertical problems. We then rounded a corner and came face to face with the beginning of the high problems the place was named for.

Countless 30 to 40 foot classic pockmarked faces and arêtes, most vertical and some slightly overhanging, stretch through the forest for a few hundred yards. Scoping out the top for possible anchor sites, I was elated to find three coldshuts placed right above the long face we had decided to toprope! But my joy lasted only a short while as a group of bees mistook my out-of-place purple shorts and multicolored shirt for pollen central, and I limped away in pain, having been stung for the first time in my life almost simultaneously by three bastard bees.

Still wincing in discomfort from the stings, we roped up for a stunning vertical to slightly overhanging pocketfest about 35 feet high. It was a moderate classic, but so were dozens of other problems at Tall Boys. We did some more, shorter problems, finished off with some severe bouldering, then headed back to our campsite at Big Springs for chili dogs and ice cold beverages.

Sunday morning we awoke to ice on our dirty pots and pans at our campsite. Slowly sipping hot beverages, we stood around the revived campfire and debated where to climb for the day. Our planned destination, Clark Canyon, was scrapped as we decided we wanted a site both a little closer to the campsite and less crowded. We settled on the obvious compromise, a place called The Stumps.

The Stumps is located about three miles on dirt roads from Big Springs campground. Forming the walls of a tremendous natural amphitheater, The Stumps consists of three main crags of mostly traditional crack climbing with a few scattered bolt ladder sport climbs. We chose the first crag on the left, which offered us five routes ranging from 5.9 to 5.10b. The approach was hideous, up steep, loose, pumice-covered slopes. But the magnificent setting more than made up for the ugly approach.

Did I say earlier that Tall Boys was the twin sibling of Deadman's Summit? Let me clarify: The Stumps is the twin of Deadman's, and Tall Boys is merely a cousin. The Stumps features the same polished volcanic faces as Deadman's, with a similar concentration of letterbox holds and near lack of lichen. But where Deadman's routes may reach only up to 30 to 35 feet tall, routes of similar quality but 60 to 80 feet tall are not uncommon at The Stumps.

Matt set two bomber topropes that gave us access to all five routes. We dove straight in, attempting *Free Burning* 5.10b * (TR) as our "warm up." It's a wickedly steep, unrelenting face chock full of a mixture of the trademarked sharp and sloping letterbox holds. Matt made impressive progress on two attempts, the consistent severity of the route spitting him off about two thirds of the way up. I got about a third of the way up before mental failure: preparing to dyno for a slot high above my head, I spotted what appeared to be bright red lichen on the top of the hold. It turned out to be Matt's blood, fresh and dripping from a sharp fang on the top of the slot. The vampire hold would not claim a second victim of the day. That was enough for me to say bye-bye to *Free Burning*.

We spent the rest of the morning toproping routes such as *Orange Zigzag*, 5.9 **, a very nice hand/fist crack, and *Roll 'em Easy*, 5.9 *, another crack which was among the easier routes we tried because it was one of the rare Stumps routes offering some nice resting spots on the way up. Most routes at The Stumps are continuous, unrelenting pumpers.

I wanted in a bad way to crank *Knucklenutz*, 5.10a **, a beautiful 50 foot finger crack, but reconsidered when I saw the beehive inside the crack towards the bottom. Still swollen from my misadventures in bee-land at Tall Boys, and not willing to risk further disfigurement (not to mention pain) in the name of a fine line, I decided to leave it for another day. We must come back next summer: to tick *Free Burning* after working more endurance on long, pumpy routes; and to tick *Knucklenutz*, assuming the bees and/or my fears of their kind are gone.

Back at camp in Big Springs for some rest and relaxation, it wasn't long before Matt, Christian, and I had grabbed shoes and chalk bags and gone for a "stroll." Downstream from the campground, the south side sported some big rocks, but the north side was tempting us with some smaller rocks that might hold some potential for good bouldering. Within an hour or two, we had created five or six pumpy jugfests, repeating most of them several times. A deer and two fawns watched from about a hundred feet away, wondering why these strange creatures were heaving themselves up rock faces and making strange grunting noises. Finished, we hobbled back to camp totally worked and ready to scarf. There's no rest for the wicked on a road trip.

Matt and Christian borrowed my car keys and headed down to Mammoth to replenish our dwindling supply of beverages. Bob and Joice rounded up all remaining scraps and morsels of food, assembling the most incredible stew ever concocted. I tended the fire, enjoying my last evening of this Sierra road trip.

As the stew disappeared and the brew wore thin, the air turned cold and we huddled closer to the fire for warmth as we swapped stories. The subject matter wavered violently, from friends and coworkers, to routes tried and sometimes completed, to wild events factual or fictitious. Matt, a former hang gliding instructor, told us of the annual parties thrown by hang glider pilots where they would throw an old hang glider into the fire as a sacrifice to appease the hang gliding gods.

Looking back, it had been a wonderful trip. I had found some new places to climb, learned some new tricks, and spent some time with new friends. The climbing gods had smiled kindly on us. Returning the favor, I threw my trusty old locking carabiner into the fire. We all watched intently as it began to glow, then quickly twisted and contorted, dripping molten metal down into the fire. And as quickly as it had started, it was all over. Too quickly.

What About B.O.B.?
Mountain Bikes and Cash Crops in the San Bernardino Mountains

This story first ran in issue #77 (02.15.00) of Dirt Rag magazine. While it is purely speculation the guys with the trailers were the same ones responsible for the pot farm, all of the events in this story did actually occur.

The first time I heard the term B.O.B., Clem and I were discussing a planned five-day mountain bike extravaganza across Santa Catalina Island. He explained how a "Beast of Burden"—a one-wheeled mountain bike trailer—might come in handy for hauling around essentials on the dirt roads. I envisioned the mountain bike version of a fifth wheel, the perfect place to stash important stuff like tent, sleeping bag, filet mignon, smoking jacket, and six packs of choice microbrew. "Roughing it" instantly took on an entirely different meaning.

Only a few days later, I saw my first B.O.B.—actually a pack of four of them, about a block from home. On the daily grind up the hill to clean my favorite singletrack, suddenly four mountain bikers appeared coming down, each towing an unusual-looking one-wheeled trailer. Each trailer carried a rather large, tightly secured load. My amazement at the multiple B.O.B. sighting quickly gave way to close examination, as something about these dudes was not quite right. Four bikers, just coming off the mountain, carrying big loads—obviously, they had come far. Maybe all the way from Big Bear? No, even that journey wouldn't require an overnighter, being about 20 to 25 miles on fire roads and jeep trails, and the majority of it downhill.

Their bulging loads were carefully concealed under small tarps held tight with bungee cords, not giving me the slightest hint as to what they may have been carrying. Perhaps my suspicions were driven by memories of my own guilt. I remembered about eight years prior, when Jeff and I rode into the same area on our mountain bikes, me hauling a "kid trailer" with a backpack strapped in the seatbelt and a child's helmet propped on top to look vaguely like a kid. We kept yelling back to our faux child, "Are you O.K. back there, Amanda?," trying hard not to laugh. But it was all a clever ruse to get up into the orange groves and liberate 100 pounds of ripe oranges from the oppressive citrus farmers of East Highlands. We hauled the oranges down in the trailer and had fresh-squeezed orange juice for several days, until we could no longer stomach the thought of it.

Maybe the B.O.B. crew was up to something similar. I tried to imagine orange-sized bumps revealing the secret payload under their tarps, but to no avail. Then I noticed their attire: baggy shorts and t-shirts. While this was indeed my mountain biking wardrobe of choice, it was not what I'd imagine from hard-core dudes each pulling a personalized B.O.B. No helmets or gloves either, which seemed highly inappropriate for their obviously lengthy journey. This was getting real strange.

As they passed close enough for a greeting, I attempted to exchange pleasantries with my mountain bike brethren, but was not obliged with even momentary eye contact, let alone a return "howzit"... A serious breach of mountain bike etiquette; the bastards had snubbed me! Just then, the loser in the lead awkwardly blew his right foot out of his toe clip and almost bit the pavement. Amateur! Just what the hell was going on?

And with a flash of dirt-encrusted metal, they were gone. I continued up the hill, figuratively scratching my head for a moment or two. But the B.O.B. incident was quickly filed to memory as I became entranced by the rhythm of the uphill grind, then the liquid-like flow through the twisting singletrack, followed by the rush of air against my face as I accelerated quickly down the exit fire road.

Southern California's East Highlands area used to be the Orange Basket of the United States. Forget "Orange County", and forget Florida. This place was once the undisputed king. Enough fiber left the fertile loins of the Inland Empire to keep half the world regular through the next millennium. But alas, it was not meant to be. Diseased rootstock was used for the majority of the trees, and they started dying. Highland and nearby Redlands still sport stands of citrus groves, but they are a mere shadow of the greatness which once was.

In addition to the climate being just right for growing citrus, there was also a readily available source of water nearby—the San Bernardino Mountains. Nestled on a rough plateau between the mountains and the valley, Highland has first dibs on the cool, clear runoff from the mountains.

Getting water down the mountain and to the groves may sound simple enough, but in fact demanded miraculous (for the time) feats of engineering. Flumes (rock and cement-lined trenches), and later buried pipes, plucked the sweet water from its source high in the canyons, then snaked their way for miles down the foothills for distribution amongst the thirsty groves. A break high in the distribution system could spell disaster, as it might go unnoticed for some time.

The flumes were built long before cars "blessed" the area with noxious fumes, wide roads, and other destructive influences. So the flumes were monitored and maintained on foot, on trails built alongside them. To this day, many of these footpaths remain as the only access to the aging flume system. More recently, a few hard-core mountain bikers have discovered that these trails make for kick-ass singletrack.

Plunge Creek has three distinct identities. Lower Plunge Creek is a beautiful riparian setting, reached from my house by a mile-long flat ride on horse trails and dirt roads—a favorite when I take my kids on a ride. Middle Plunge Creek follows an open flume for a while before it is transformed into a singletrack death wish—imagine a half-foot-wide, sloping, hardscrabble trail where one false move means 60 feet of air, followed by a sudden stop in a few inches of water. It's something a sane person might only try once in their lifetime (I've done it twice in eight years...and swear, never again). But if you're looking for great local singletrack that's challenging but you'll have a great chance of surviving, Upper Plunge Creek is the destination of choice.

The entry is a harsh uphill two miles on a steep and sometimes sandy dirt road, then a quick little turn to the right that you might easily miss if you didn't know exactly where to look—the start of the singletrack. Most people really enjoy the first two or three miles of singletrack on the Upper Plunge Creek trail. It's generally well-maintained, although it has its fair share of washouts and hike-a-bikes. It follows an old buried clay pipe that contours around the mountain as it makes its way down from high up the mountain. The pipe features intermittent breather holes—holes which make for interesting obstacles, all the more strange because of the huge sucking sounds they sometimes make as you whisk by.

It can be an immensely peaceful ride. Far from the noise of the suburbs, you hear the occasional jet fly overhead, but mostly you hear yourself gasping for air, your heart pounding heavy in your chest, and your bike straining against the dirt and loose stone.

I once saw a bobcat on this trail, and have seen the footprints of many deer. A few months ago, a rattlesnake rattled violently behind a bush, just inches from our feet as Dave, Clem, Mike, and I descended. I've never actually seen a mountain lion up there, although others have. Add to that the sheer drops of 100 to 200 feet off the side of the trail in spots, and it really adds a sense of adventure to the place. If something happened, it's rugged enough that they might never find your body.

A significant landmark along the trail is affectionately known as "The Jacuzzi"—a large, deep, square stone holding tank where the water collects momentarily before resuming its controlled plunge down the mountain. But don't let the nickname fool you; The Jacuzzi is ice cold, and it's not something you'd ever want to swim in. The water is dirty, and the suction caused by the water flowing into the exit pipe is probably strong enough to rip your arm off. The last time I was there, I noticed a piece of PVC pipe and an empty bag of chemical fertilizer lying next to The Jacuzzi. I hypothesized that workers from the groves miles below may have carried the fertilizer up the long trail and poured it into The Jacuzzi to let it dissolve into the water for better dispersion down below, but it seemed like a long shot. And I still had no plausible explanation of why someone would walk several miles into no man's land carrying a 10-foot section of PVC pipe.

Helicopters were unusual enough in the neighborhood that whenever I heard one, I'd make an effort to watch it. In late August, I noticed a huge increase in local air traffic; several helicopters a day buzzed the hills to the north and the east, following a flight path I had never noticed before. This continued unabated for about two weeks, and then abruptly stopped. A short time later, I was reading the newspaper before my morning ride, and the headline screamed out: *Record Pot Bust in Mountains.*

Working on an anonymous tip, San Bernardino County Sheriff's Deputies and U.S. Forest Service officials had located a large pot farm in the San Bernardino Mountains. Water siphoned from a nearby irrigation pipeline guaranteed the place a constant supply of water. The location was so isolated, if law enforcement had not received the anonymous tip, the farm surely could have operated unnoticed for years. The location: Upper Plunge Creek.

In less than a month, Sheriff's Deputies had raided three more pot farms within ten miles of Plunge Creek. In all, nearly 50,000 pot plants, with a street value of more than $150 million, were seized. Officials say the combination of near complete isolation in close proximity to civilization with a readily available water supply makes the canyons behind the orange groves an idyllic location for the growing of California's number one cash crop. All four of the pot farms were linked when officers noticed similar looking bags of chemical fertilizer at each location and checked the serial numbers. Turns out they were from the same batch at the same manufacturing plant.

At one of the farms, officers found two armed Mexican nationals, living in a well-stocked camp featuring all the accouterments, including a tomato and jalapeno pepper garden—all the fixin's for fresh salsa. And the caretakers had spent hundreds of man-hours cutting a new trail through two miles of impenetrable chaparral—future singletrack!

The PVC pipe. The empty bag of fertilizer. The pieces of the puzzle were starting to fit together. But what about the B.O.B.s? Just what were those guys carrying under those tarps anyway?

The Boneyard

This story was previously published in Boulderfest! The Snow Valley Bouldering Guide (2005).

I ditched out of work early, not uncommon behavior on a summer afternoon. Redlands gets so hot in the summer, and Snow Valley is so cool. It's even cooler when you have the whole place to yourself.

So there I was, minding my own business, working a new bouldering area in Snow Valley Central (The Wasteland to be specific). Like I usually do after I get tired, I packed up the shoes and went exploring. There's always another boulder waiting to be plucked from the fertile loins of Snow Valley, and I'm a pluckin' fool.

I had long had my eye on a clump of boulders south of The Old Man formation, just north of Highway 18. We'd all walked by them dozens of times. I asked a few people. Nobody in the Snow Valley crew had ever been down there. May 20th, 1999 happened to be the day I finally wandered down to check them out.

They were nothing spectacular. A dozen or two boulder problems. A few of them might even be pretty good. The highlight of the visit was wandering between a couple small boulders and finding a nearly complete backbone lying on top of some decaying oak leaves.

I'm no doctor, and I don't play one on TV, but I did take quite a few senior and graduate level anthropology and biology classes in college. Much like a cheap prostitute, I've been around a lot of bones. While I can't positively identify human remains, I couldn't rule these out as being human, either. I chalked it up to the Snow Valley experience, and only let it creep me out for a few minutes. Then I forgot about it and kept exploring.

Always in search of new stone, I ended up finding a new cross-country route between The Old Man and The Indifferent Boulders, scouting a number of promising clumps of boulders along the way. I slept well that night; I was tired, and the bones were completely forgotten.

Until the next morning at work, that is. I mentioned it to someone, and they freaked. Then I asked a coworker who for many years was a local Chief of Police. He said it was unlikely that it was human, but I should call the Sheriff just in case. Just so I could sleep at night. And in case it was human, so that the family of the victim could finally get some closure.

That afternoon I bailed on my son's Little League game, met the detective at the station about 5 p.m., and we headed over to Snow Valley. The coolest part was that we got to park right on the side of the road very close to where the bones were. The adjoining highway is "no parking," and getting to The Old Man area usually requires a 15 minute hike from the Snow

Valley East or Snow Valley West parking areas. With valet parking, it took all of 45 seconds to relocate the bones.

The detective studied them, took some photos, and then put the specimen in a bag to take back to the lab. He couldn't rule out the possibility, either. He took out some spray paint and marked the boulders nearby. One of the most chilling things I've ever seen in my life was when the detective stood where the bones were, on these large, thin plates that had exfoliated from the nearby boulders, and started wiggling them with his feet. Whatever was underneath the rocks, it made a horrible "squishing" sound. I looked at his face, and it was almost pure white. "I don't like the sound of this..." he said. We decided to get the hell out of there.

Back at the car, he spent a long time thanking me. It likely wasn't human, but I did the right thing in calling it in. "There are hundreds of dead bodies up here we haven't found yet," he said. Yikes, there's a sobering statistic. I offered to remove The Old Man area from the Snow Valley Web site and post a message asking people to stay away until the issue was resolved, and he thought that was a good idea. He said he would call me as soon as he got the results back from the lab work.

In mid July, 1999, Jay Kim and I went bouldering at Snow Valley West. Being fat and weak, after a couple hours we burnt out, and decided to leave early. The cold brews waiting back home in my fridge were calling our names. An hour later, sitting in my backyard, drinking beers and doing tequila shots, the phone rang. It was the detective. After identifying himself, he said simply, "Pig or lamb." "Wow," I replied, "I expected almost anything, but I never would have guessed that." He thanked me again, and we said goodbye.

Pig or lamb. Jay, with a degree in forensic psychology, immediately shouted "ritual sacrifice!" I tend to think maybe there was a party of some kind at the Snow Valley Lodge, and an animal got the remains out of the trash can and drug them down the road.

Whatever. At least it wasn't some dead guy.

Back in the Saddle

This is a short piece I wrote when Dirt Rag magazine contacted me in early 2002 to see if I had anything new to submit. They never used it.

It was hard to get back into a routine after the tragic events of Sept. 11th. That fateful morning, I had put on my riding clothes, and turned on the TV for a quick glimpse at the weather report. Instead of some inept weatherman saying "partly cloudy with highs in the mid to lower 80's", I saw the unforgettable images that forever changed our way of life.

Yet I still went riding that morning. It wasn't much fun, though. I got a late start because of the distractions on the TV. And by the time I got up in the hills, a construction crew was already going full bore. After about 20 minutes of dodging heavy equipment and trying to find the remains of my favorite singletrack, I called it a day.

The next three hours were spent in front of the TV, watching the unfolding drama as buildings collapsed and scores of innocent people lost their lives. I sat there on my couch, watching my color TV, in my riding clothes, sipping from my water bottle, and was overwhelmed by destruction — the destruction of the World Trade Center, and, more locally, the destruction of the mountain bike playground in the hills behind my house.

After that earth-shattering day, I couldn't find the motivation to ride for a while. When I finally did, the experience was only slightly better than mediocre. Of course, it was good to once again feel the wind against my face and breathe in the fragrance of the hills. But the familiar rhythm that typically characterizes my morning rides somehow remained elusive. I began to wonder if the world could ever be the same again.

I got back on my bike the other day. A few months to put everything in perspective, a change of clothes, and a change of scenery did wonders. A few minutes into the ride, the familiar feeling was back, in all its glory. A few miles later, the world was as it should be. The events of the last five months were not forgotten, but revered.

The freedoms we have—be they as basic as democracy, or as esoteric as the right to ride down a choice piece of singletrack— are too precious to take for granted. Be it nineteen guys with jumbo jets, or one guy with a bulldozer, they can shake our freedoms, but they can't take them away.

And while I was out, I found this incredible new singletrack...

Fiction

The Black Death Interview
"Mad" Joe Jiminez, Founder and President of Black Death Mountain Bikes

A cynical, wickedly funny mock-interview, sort of a "This is Spinal Tap" take on the mountain bike industry, this story originally ran in issue #74 (08.15.99) of Dirt Rag magazine.

A few days ago, I picked up the latest issue of some corporate mountain biking mag, and spent an hour drooling over all the high-priced, super-light-weight components. We've come a long way. But have we come too far, too fast? My interview with "Mad" Joe Jiminez, founder and president of Black Death Mountain Bikes, left me thinking—is our obsession with the latest frames and lightest components healthy for the sport of mountain biking?

Matt Artz (MA): When did you first get involved in mountain biking?

"Mad" Joe Jiminez (JJ): Having been introduced to the sport in 1987, I bought one of the real early Murray "enthusiast" mountain bikes, and I've been riding like hell on cheap-ass bikes ever since.

MA: What are you riding right now?

JJ: I currently alternate between two Black Death bikes — a hardtail, and a full suspension bike — but they are not anything to be envied by anyone. When out riding by myself, it doesn't matter; I'm having fun, getting exercise, and experiencing mother nature at her best. When riding with friends, who will inevitably have more money invested in their bikes than I do in my car, I'm usually O.K. because they judge me on my riding ability, not the purchase price of my stead. But when reading about all those new half-ounce components costing more than a three-bedroom house, that's when I started feeling the most insecure. My penis shrinks to half its normal size. The ultimate case of pee-pee envy.

MA: How did you decide to start your own mountain bike company?

JJ: The bike envy was really distracting me. It wasn't what you think — it wasn't jealousy. It was more like frustration with the absurdity of the situation. Then one day in 1995 it dawned on me. This is America, damn it! When confronted with adversity or injustice, what's a red blooded American to do? Write my congressman? No, they all accept hefty campaign contributions from bike manufacturers, and I'd be lucky to get a derogatory form letter response. Organize a sit-in? No, that's so 70's; besides, a one-man sit-in would be about as productive as pissing in the wind. No, in the true spirit of our great country, I needed to accept the situation — then find some way to make a buck off it! Thus, I decided to find a way to turn my frustrations into a profitable business. I love this country!

MA: Did you write a business plan?

JJ: F&*k no! Like most wannabe entrepreneurs with a half-ass idea, I spent most of my time not on developing a business plan or product prototypes. No, I invested countless hours of effort in what matters most: coming up with a cool company name, slogan, and logo!

MA: O.K., I'll bite. How did you decide to name your company "Black Death"?

JJ: It has many meanings. I thought I had the bubonic plague in 1994, after a trip to the Eastern Sierra (where many areas have since been closed because of infected rodents), and I did a lot of reading about it. It was horrible. I thought I was dying. I had to register with the county health department, and go through all these tests. You know, with the plague, it's usually fatal within 7 to 10 days. And the f&*king county health department didn't give me the test results for four weeks. Maybe that f&*ked me up for life.

MA: What about the slogan?

JJ: Slogans are important, maybe even more important than the company name. So I had a little contest among my close friends. The prize was a six pack. Some of the more memorable slogans I got from my friends were:

- "Black Death: All the rage in Europe, now coming to America!"
- "Black Death: Once you go black, you'll never go back."
- "Black Death: The Perfect Bike for the Afterlife."

- "Black Death: Like Death, it ain't pretty."
- "Black Death: When nothing else matters."
- "Black Death: Where do you want to die today?"

But in the end, the choice was pretty simple: "Nothing says 'I don't give a shit' like a Black Death Mountain Bike." Since this was one of my own, not only did I come up with a great slogan, but I got to drink the sixer solo.

MA: I've actually seen your logo on some t-shirts worn by dirt bag mountain bikers in Southern California.

JJ: Yep. I decided on the Grim Reaper, riding his trusty mountain bike side saddle. After all, the Grim Reaper wears a dress, and at Black Death Mountain Bikes, chivalry is not dead.

MA: Can you describe your design principles?

JJ: Sure. It's pretty simple. Our philosophy is to pump out a few simple, cheap bikes. The emphasis is on riding, not spending tons of money posing. If you're a real mountain biker, it's all about riding, not how much your bike cost. Is it just me who thinks that a $3,000 bike is like an anorexic movie star? For me, the bigger the cushion, the sweeter the pushin'.

MA: And your manufacturing process?

JJ: O.K., so you're asking for our trade secrets? (laughs) You know, you can get a really good mountain bike for about $150 to $200 these days if you know where to look. That would be K-Mart, Wal-Mart, Toys-R-Us. You'd be surprised what you can get for this price these days: 21 speed, Shimano components, hardtail, and sometimes even full suspension! Sure, they're not of the highest quality, shall we say. And sure, they weigh more than the fat lady at the circus. But they're mountain bikes, damn it, and they look really cool. The biggest problem is, sadly, that the "Murray" or "Huffy" stickers will get you laughed off the local singletrack. So at Black Death, we provide you with a cheap bike that's not easily recognizable as a piece of crap. I won't go into details, but let's just say our primary tools are razor blades for scraping off stickers, and we buy cans of black spray paint by the case.

MA: So you're saying you don't make anything yourself, you OEM everything?

JJ: OEM? I think I know what that means... Uh, yeah, we OEM everything.

MA: And your frames?

JJ: We'll use any frame we can find in the trash, at garage sales, Goodwill,...

MA: Uh, no, I meant, steel, chromoly, aluminum...

JJ: Yeah, I know what you meant. You don't find a lot of aluminum or titanium frames for $10 at the Salvation Army, you know. Besides, nothing beats steel. It lasts a long time, takes a licking, and it breathes well.

MA: Breathes well? Um ... next question. With all the opportunities in this market, why have you not expanded your business as rapidly as some of the other bike manufacturers?

JJ: I realized that becoming part of the corporate food chain would go against every instinct that made me react so negatively to that special issue of such-and-suck magazine. I wouldn't have time to ride; I'd have a $3,000 bike that would just collect dust in my garage. I'd get big, and someone like Schwinn would try to buy me out; all those millions in cash would surely corrupt my morals and make me do evil things. Speaking of cash, I also realized with my bad credit record, I had absolutely no chance of getting a loan to finance my fledgling company. And I still had no business plan, and no real ideas for products. Add all this together, and it was looking pretty grim. I was almost regretting having turned in my two week notice at McDonalds.

In the end, I decided to keep it going, but in a small way. Although the prospects for success looked grim, I'd give it a whirl. After all, I had the killer name for a company! Black Death Mountain Bikes couldn't fail me! Like many underachievers with mediocre ideas before me, I decided to go grassroots, keep it small, and avoid the ulcers.

Many people have lost sight of the real reason you buy that hunk of metal and rubber in the first place. Thanks to the influences of big corporate mountain biking, too many people who should be saying "Biking is my life" are now saying "My bike is my life." That's really sad, man. Think about that.

MA: So what exactly makes a Black Death Mountain Bike stand out from the crowd?

JJ: The key is the paint job. O.K., so here's a trade secret. Want a Black Death paint job? Forget about all that "powder coat" bullshit. Go to your local True Value hardware store and buy a can or two of the cheapest flat black spray paint you can find. This is important: it must be FLAT black. Remember, there is no glossy finish to death. It's all black, baby. If you've got the time, remove all the parts; if not, a quick masking job with tape and newspaper will more than suffice. When doing the actual spraying, please remember that drips and runs are not to be avoided; in fact, if at all possible, go out of your way to make these "flaws," which show that you really don't give a shit. In the industry, we call it "ideological camouflage."

MA: So do you think people today over-accessorize their bikes?

JJ: Hell yes! It's a joke. An over-accessorized bike looks about as attractive as a cheap prostitute. Leave the blue eye shadow at home tonight, baby. You'll get more business.

MA: What about clothing... ?

JJ: Forget the dumb jerseys and pants and other stuff which cost more than your bike. To ride a Black Death Mountain Bike, you've got to dress correctly, in Team Black Death-approved attire. In the summer, its cut-off 501s and a groovy tie-die cotton t-shirt. For more severe winter conditions, it's cut-off 501s, a groovy tie-die cotton t-shirt, and a hip flask of Jack Daniels.

MA: But I thought you were currently in the process of expanding your business and starting your own clothing line?

JJ: Hey, man, how else is a person supposed to make a buck, much less run a company in the black, with a grassroots program aimed at destroying corporate mountain biking? The answer is one word, exclaimed by Mel Brooks in the movie "Spaceballs"—Merchandising! That's right, coming soon to a store near you, Black Death Mountain Biking t-shirts! The resemblance to Grateful Dead merchandise is only coincidental. And if a guy's got to make a buck, it's more conscionable to do it selling bad clothing, than to do it by destroying a sport enjoyed by so many people today.

MA: It really isn't about the money with you, is it?

JJ: If everyone out there follows my lead, we can start a revolution, man. While technological advances in equipment design are good for the sport, the rampant materialism of biking consumers, if left unchecked, may one day lead to the death of mountain biking's soul. That's sad.

MA: Do you think frenzied materialism will really destroy the sport of mountain biking as we know it today?

JJ: You mean it hasn't already? (laughs) Seriously, for many people, mountain biking has already changed from a super-fun pastime, to that thing you do to justify the purchase of all that cool stuff you need to purchase to be in with the in crowd, keep up with the Joneses, and make up for all your inadequacies as a human. Jesus Christ, if we're not careful, mountain biking could go the way of skiing! Imagining the trendy post-Yuppies wearing expensive biking outfits while sipping designer coffees at the lodge of the mountain biking park, while their $6,000 bikes are parked outside collecting dust, isn't that big of a stretch. I mean, have you been to Mammoth lately?

MA: In your opinion, what can be done to save the sport?

JJ: In order to save for our children and grandchildren the joys of riding a beautiful slice of singletrack without worrying about whether you've got the "right" forks or the "best" headset according to the latest swagazine, we need to make a statement. Black Death is not just a company, it's really a statement. Unless we all get back to the basics, we'll all wake up one day and the plague of gear obsession will have killed the soul of the sport we love most. Then all that will be left is golf.

MA: What can the average mountain biker do to help?

JJ: Get yourself a cheap-ass mountain bike and ride it. Ride like the wind. Ride like today is your last day on earth. Ride like any other cliché you can think of. But just ride. After all, that's what it's all about. Everything else is just posing.

Of Spicy Meatloaf, Blackened Voodoo, and the Life of a Leo

This beer review gone psycho was originally published in the Winter 1999 (Volume 3, Issue 4) issue of TopRope magazine, as well as on ClimbingChannel.com in 2000.

Once upon a time, in a public restroom far, far away, a man birthed a plan that just might change his life, as well as the lives of millions of others. The plan: a road trip to the Eastern Sierra. The man: me.

It began after a particularly bad but not totally unexpected run-in with the meatloaf and gravy at Peg's Diner in San Bernardino. Thankfully, the stall was unoccupied, there was an extra roll of toilet paper handy, and the container of ass gaskets screwed to the wall was fully stocked. I settled in for the long, unpleasant haul, the latest issue of *TopRope* magazine on my lap for moral support. After a few awful minutes, I stumbled upon Jonathon Weed's horoscopes on page 7, and read mine.

> Leo: Embark on an adventure with someone you can't stand-the relationship grows worse. Inspiration comes to you in the bathroom. You may learn a little something about meatloaf.

Coincidence? I think not. No, it was destiny of cosmic proportions. I had the inspiration down, thanks to my forsaken location and the diuretic equivalent of an epiphany on meatloaf; now all I needed was a road trip with an undesirable climbing partner, and then the self-fulfilling prophesy would fully fulfill itself.

For this trip I would need a truly obnoxious partner, one who I would hopefully never speak to again after it was all over. The answer came instantly, and was so repulsive that my bowels again opened violently in a valiant yet futile attempt to reverse the inevitable choice: Lanny Limberg, or as we like to call him behind his back, "The Mouth."

The best thing about The Mouth was that he was filthy rich, at least relatively speaking. He'd be happy to tag along, and in return for putting up with his incessant babble, I would make him pay for gas, brew, and Taco Bell.

Now The Mouth was loaded because somebody in his family knocked off and left a fortune behind. Vanity being the most significant of his many character flaws, he was always presenting his well-offness as a result of some fantastic investment scheme, while in reality his main skill set consisted entirely of belching the alphabet without taking a breath and driving his leased BMW to the bank to make withdrawals from the trust fund. Over the years, his stories got ever more elaborate and implausible, taking on an increasing air of desperation as the balance of the trust fund inched closer and closer to $0.00.

I picked The Mouth up at 5:30 p.m., and we drove immediately to the ATM. A stop at the gas station to top off the tank, then across town to the liquor store with the specialty beers—hey, he was going to pay in advance for my mental anguish—and we were off to The Buttermilks.

The plan was to hit the dirt parking lot next to the Birthday Boulders by 11 p.m., drink a few beers, get to sleep, then wake up early for a three to four hour bouldering session, get some Taco Bell in Bishop, and drive home. While ten hours of driving may seem extreme for only a few hours of bouldering, remember that the company was truly repulsive. And since my horoscope didn't specify exactly how much time I needed to spend with my mental nemesis in order to fulfill the prophesy, I could get out quickly and still complete my cosmic destiny. Plus, five minutes of bouldering at The Buttermilks is easily worth ten hours of hell.

"Lanny, you're gonna love this beer we—uh, you—bought," I said. "Blackened Voodoo is from New Orleans, it's dark and it's lovely. Almost like maple syrup. It just may be the most perfect beer ever brewed on the planet."

"Two six packs, man, that was over twenty bucks for beer just for one night...we aren't really going to drink all of that, are we?"

"Hey, man," I retorted, "can you really put a price on perfection? Besides, well, at The Buttermilks, you often hook up with other climbers squatting in the parking lot for the night, and you need to bring enough to share." Sensing his discomfort with the tab, I decided to prey on his vanity.

Speaking in a calm, soothing voice, I added "Besides, if anyone can afford the finer things in life, it's you, right my friend?"

Sheer genius. It immediately cut off all resistance at the knees. There would be no more talk of extravagant beverage expenditures that night; no, instead I had painted myself into a corner, and now had to listen to his latest faux investment ramblings.

"Speaking of which," he clumsily segued, "there's this new stock—well, it's not actually a stock yet, they're going to do an IPO soon—anyway, it's called KidKorp, some new e-commerce site where they don't actually inventory anything at all, they only broker the sales, simply passing the sale on to the supplier who delivers direct to the client, while KidKorp collects the standard 15% margin...think of it as the Amazon.com for diapers and baby formula..."

For a bullshit artist, The Mouth was pretty good. But I wasn't bad myself. I tuned out, hypnotized by the road, reliving the sequences of my favorite Buttermilk boulder problems like little movies in my head, all the while maintaining a pseudo-conversation with The Mouth by simply plucking single words from his monologue and parroting them back as questions. "IPO?" I mock asked. "15%, huh?" I pretended to verify. My body appeared to be engaged in the conversation, but my mind was pulling hard on Buttermilk granite.

We pulled in to the lot about 11:20 p.m., and I opened the ice chest. "Tradition, man," I improvised. "The first night out at The Buttermilks, you just throw back a few while you watch the stars. Enjoy the silence, brother." I thought my use of the term brother particularly clever here; if he protested, he separated himself from the brotherhood, alienating himself from all climbing kind. It would be road trip suicide, a serious breach of protocol, and there was no way he could do it.

Much beer was consumed and few words were spoken. For a lightweight not used to mass quantities of dark beer, he downed his fair share of The Voodoo. I have no idea who passed out first.

6:10 a.m., the sun was just breaking over the top of The Whites to the East, casting that otherworldly translucent orange glow over the Sierra Crest to the west. "Get up, man, it's time to climb!" I yelled into Lanny's left ear. His eyes opened, connecting with mine, and then he rolled on to his right side and puked on his sleeping bag. Shit. Blackened Voodoo had cast its ugly spell on The Mouth. Oh well, I had my crash pad and could handle it myself.

Surprisingly, there were two Blackened Voodoos left in the ice chest—breakfast of champions! I downed one quickly, and stowed the other in my pack to drink under the *Iron Man Traverse* as I put on my shoes and performed my elaborate pre-bouldering taping ritual.

Fueled by The Voodoo and boosted by the unanticipated absence of my partner, I spent several hours running from boulder to boulder, throwing my body violently against the sharp stone, experiencing the best that East Side bouldering has to offer. By 10:30 a.m., it was getting a bit toasty, my forearms felt like baked hams, and an unbelievable stench rose from my climbing shoes. Funny, after a few Blackened Voodoos, the shoes smelled vaguely of meatloaf. My lower intestine rumbled violently in protest. Don't worry, baby, I reassured my bowels; it's not a flashback of the Thursday Blue Plate Special at Peg's, just an unfortunate coincidence.

I headed back to the car to check Lanny's corpse for a pulse, storing my rancid shoes safely in my pack before I got within range of his nostrils. Hey, watching guys puke is damn funny, but I was looking at a five hour car ride through the desert with this guy.

The Mouth was doing better, just weak in the knees and wanting badly to bail. I obliged, and we skipped the Taco Bell stop on the way down. We stopped only for gas in Bishop, where The Mouth bought a bottle of water and some soda crackers, while I picked up a bag of spicy pork rinds, a large Diet Coke, and a small box of Ho Ho's.

The ride back was fairly uneventful, Lanny gasping for air with his head hanging out the window as I headbanged to Metallica's "Kill 'em All" and KISS "Destroyer." I dropped The Mouth off around 4:30 p.m., and never saw him again. I don't think it was a conscious decision by either party to avoid each other; it's just the way it worked out.

Or maybe it was destiny.

The Stone Apocalypse
Episode One:
Every Journey has a Beginning

A slightly different version of this story was first published in the issue #27 (February 1999) of What's the Beta?

The lights shot past in a Technicolor blur, transforming my four-cylinder import into a rebel ship for a few brief seconds. I was Luke Skywalker, and the horn was my laser cannon, blastin' the enemy until the semi driver flashed his lights and I came to. The heater was on high, lending an acrid, half-baked tinge to the smell of diesel, body odor, and dried blood. Ninety minutes since we had left Merve's dank apartment in West Hollywood, and I was already questioning my sanity for setting out on this journey. Doing his part to keep me awake, my partner snored loudly in the passenger seat, as I beat my head against the drivers' window in time to "TV Set" by The Cramps.

> *I see you on my TV set*
> *I see you on my TV set*
> *I cut your head off and stick it in my TV set*
> *I use your eyeballs for knobs on my TV set*

Lyrics like that, especially when backed up by fuzzy surf guitar playing riffs of mail-order magnitude, brought out the best in me. No doubt about it, we were on the road now! We were heading towards Mecca, for some of the best bouldering this side of nirvana. Although only for a day, Joshua Tree would be the perfect prelude to my quest for the meaning of life.

The rear of the car sagged low, nearly touching the ground, dragging along the highway like the pock-marked ass of a scared hyena as it makes a hasty retreat across the deserted plains of the Serengeti. In the trunk, under the optional gear like sleeping bag and clean underwear, the ice chest was filled with six half gallons of fine microbrew, just chillin'. We had brought along four pint glasses—one for me, one for Merve, and two emergency backups in case the primaries were broken in an auto accident or night of drunken revelry. Just because we were on the road, sleeping on dirt, ignoring personal hygiene, and foraging dumpsters for food scraps and grubs, didn't mean we had to lower our beverage standards and imbibe like savages. On the road, selective decadence rules.

Merve was snoring so loudly he woke himself up. He managed to blurt out "Dude, where are we?" before he drifted off again, sans answer.

My choice of company was going to make the first leg of my journey especially interesting. Not wanting to quit his lucrative career as the head "fry guy" at the local McSoy Burger, Merve was only joining me for the first overnighter of my Hajj. Perhaps he was afraid of discovering the true meaning of existence so early in his life. Or maybe he was more motivated by the scary thought of not being able to make his car payments. Whatever. To each his own, the stupid mutha.

Two hours into the drive, I was actually thankful for Merve's diligent work ethic, regardless of his motivation. Awake again, his constant mantra of "Dude, I gotta get me some pussy!" was already wearing thinner than O.J.'s claim of innocence. I could only imagine with shear horror the possibility of being on the road with him for an extended period of time. He would more than likely be the first one in the vehicle to discover the true meaning of life—first hand as it were, as I would undoubtedly be brought up on manslaughter charges in some Podunk town after smashing in his skull. Indeed, "Dude, I gotta get me some pussy!" would form the core of my insanity plea.

Merve wasn't his real name—can you imagine a parent being that cruel, to first create such a useless hunk of human flesh, then to top it off by attaching the name of "Merve" to the failed piece of performance art? I honestly didn't even know his real name. Some say it was John, others said it might have been Matthew. One guy insisted it was Noah. Suffice it to say all theories had a biblical connection. In a twisted way this all made sense. In Merve's own mind, he was a climbing God.

His full nickname, on which his faux name was based, was "Merve the Perve," as given to him by his mother somewhere in between the time of birth, and the seminal event of kicking him out of the house for sexual deviancy. Wise beyond his 18 years, he sometimes could buy beer without being carded—as long as he kept his mouth shut. Climbing with Merve was never a pleasure, as he was young, strong, and stupid, with a big fat mouth. The beta he spewed was always dead on and well delivered, but it was the other stuff he interjected that drove his climbing partners to pay extra for unlisted phone numbers. When not climbing, talking about climbing, or thinking about climbing, he was clearly out of his element.

My fake yawns—manufactured to accelerate the sleep process in Merve's brain, so I could get out of the seventy-fifth recitation of "Dude, her tits were SO BIG"—unfortunately only seemed to have the desired affect on yours truly. Merve was still going strong, pumping out his endless babble about women never had, and routes never climbed. Merve had apparently scored with thousands of women, having an on-base percentage rivaled only by the legendary Wilt Chamberlain, and more home runs than Hugh Heffner.

We finally pulled into Hidden Valley campground late, and to my surprise found a campsite quickly. My tent went up in record time, and I was almost immediately feigning sleep. With a full-on fake snore, I at least deserved a nomination—though the Oscar itself would likely go to Merve, for most valuable youngster in a supporting role.

While it was easily stupid and probably sacrilegious to be on a road trip and hit the sack without so much as the briefest of taste tests involving the lovely nectars in the ice chest, I had to take my leave of the perverted youth, lest I lose my temper and make the young boy cry. Before long, I drifted off into a deep sleep, dreaming of birds on the wing, pulling off miraculous hip shots with trusty Ole Blue.

Morning light came too quickly, but it was the unbearable smell of my own rancid flatulence that finally forced me out of my tent and into the open air. Merve must have stayed up later than me, because when the sun and I awoke, he was still sawing. With all the cunning and strategy of a lion stalking its prey through the veldt, I carefully planned my escape. I was able to extricate myself from the sleeping enclosure, change clothes, grab my gear, brush my teeth, and "rinse" with a pint of fine ale without waking The Perve.

The bouldering went well. In no hurry, I paced myself carefully. A 5.8, followed by a half hour nap in the sun. A 5.9, followed by more snooze and solar radiation. Gradually warming up, I moved on to several V0 and V1 problems, then took a nap to recharge.

It was nothing spectacular. In a way, it almost seemed like a let down—quitting my job and setting off on the road trip to find myself, and here I was on the first full day, doing laps on easy and familiar problems, hiding from a partner I couldn't stand, and not even hung over from the night before. Not quite the process of self-discovery I had planned.

A little after mid-day, Merve finally caught up with me after I grew tired of dodging him. My tips were trashed, my forearms were tired, and I was ready to drain the half-gallon of Amber I had been lugging in my pack all day. All climbed—and napped—out at this point, I hit the lukewarm brew with gusto, and prepared to play drunken spotter to the wunderkid.

Ironically, as my buzz intensified, so did Merve's level of climbing. He was strong. He was bold. He was unstoppable.

And he was stupid. Halfway up some V9 problem, I heard him whimper a feeble "Ouch," and watched him pop off the climb. He had pulled a tendon. In my brew-induced "heightened state of awareness," the only thing that saved him from further injury was the well-placed crash pad.

"Dude, I'm hosed," the pervert muttered repeatedly as we walked out, packed up camp, and aimed west. Sympathy was difficult. Although the large knot in his right index finger would mean at least a temporary delay in his rapidly advancing climbing career, the verbalization of his deep depression meant that at least I no longer had to listen to him boast of his imaginary sexual prowess on the long drive back to his apartment.

The rocks assumed shapes not of this earth as they moved by in a psychedelic dream. The Joshua trees morphed through otherworldly contortions as they bent and twisted, unnaturally pointing the way to enlightenment. Even the sky itself melted, molten globs of heaven and hell dripping onto the golden ground as shadows danced in and out of my eyeballs. Yes, it was a good trip.

Having only slightly overindulged myself on sweet barley nectar, and not having done any "real" drugs since my early twenties, I came to the startling conclusion that this was no artificially induced trip, no acid flashback, not even a cryptic sign from the gods. No, we were simply experiencing that golden moment many climbers have experienced. We were driving out of Joshua Tree National Park at sunset.

Before long, the sun was dipping below the horizon, the colors in the sky were fading faster than my buzz, and my own depression hit. I call it Josh withdrawal. Great day of climbing, excellent brew, and the most killer sunset on the planet. Never mind my poor choice of company. What else could possibly follow such a high, but a low of epic proportions. The quartz monzonite abrasions on hands and other miscellaneous body parts remind you quickly that the six layers of skin you've worn off are not extras, but there for a reason—millions of years of natural selection can't be wrong, but early man obviously wasn't a boulderer. You're also reminded of the full meaning of the word "open," when used in conjunction with the word "wound."

Ah yes, the Joshua Tree blues. But once you work through the thoughts of suicide and other only slightly less drastic measures, you become hypnotized by the headlights, entranced by the stars in the sky, mesmerized by the cool tunes emanating from the CD player...and you once again are at peace with the world. Or close enough.

The ride out, or "evacuation" as it is sometimes referred to, is a good time for introspection. Not just about the accomplishments of the trip and how they relate to your personal climbing goals. But putting the entire trip into perspective in relation to your very existence.

Alas, a summary of the day wouldn't be complete without a few words about my climbing partner. Merve the Perve, no matter how annoying he was to me and every other person he'd ever climbed with, is a master of his art. Although his social skills are weak and his personality as user friendly as a chain saw stuck in the "on" position, he has found his own inner peace through hard climbing—a peace that I, at twice his age, am still searching for. I will always envy his stupidity, er, immaturity. Immaturity leaves the mind relatively uncluttered of thoughts of failure, of the full burden of reality. I wish Merve luck in the arduous process of maturation, and hope he someday finds that pussy he's been talking about.

The end is not unlike the beginning. The lights whiz by, maybe a bit more blurred due to the mixture of dirt, chalk, and sunscreen in the eyes. Perhaps the biggest difference is the sense of partial fulfillment. Of not yet knowing the answer, but knowing you're at least a step or two closer, and enjoying the ride.

Whether it's something as complex as love, as esoteric as the perfect sandstone finger crack, as elusive as the meaning of life, or as practical as the next urinal to piss in, on the road, everybody is searching for something. Not having found mine yet, my journey would continue.

I dropped Merve off late at his run-down apartment complex. With the engine still running, I tossed his gear on the sidewalk, and mumbled something about seeing a doctor about that finger. Glad to be rid of him, I knew we would see each other again soon—perhaps after his tendon healed, and after my memory had softened the hard edges of his personality.

With newfound energy, eyes wide open and brain wide awake, I pushed the pedal to the floor and aimed my vehicle towards Arizona and enlightenment. See you in Sedona, sucka.

The Stone Apocalypse
Episode Two:
The "V" is for Vortex

A slightly different version of this story was first published in the Summer 1999 issue of Vertical Jones. In this episode, we meet "Mad" Joe Jiminez, who is also president of Black Death Mountain Bikes.

Sedona. Land of many large red rocks and one freaky human subculture. Often described in less than flattering terms as the "Malibu of Arizona," this artist's town north of Phoenix and south of Flagstaff was also the hotbed of the 1980's crystal-rubbing pseudo-religion known as "new age." And more documented alien abductions per capita than you would ever care to believe.

For sure, Sedona was one weird-ass town. The basis of the new age attraction to the area was some cosmic energy transmission bullshit, which was manifest in the Sedona area somehow differently than in other "lesser" areas of the planetary surface. These focal points of intergalactic consciousness were known as "vortexes." These vortexes attracted the fringe of society like bugs cling to a naked light bulb. I could only imagine what a vortex looked like, and had visions of cheesy special effects black holes clipped from low budget science fiction movies; of the cosmic toilet flushing, with reality spinning out of control, sucking in the minds of all the losers, freaks, and wannabe's who couldn't afford the Greyhound fare to Southern California. I had to witness a vortex for myself.

The rocks themselves were sure beautiful to look at, but as far as climbing was concerned, they were mostly mediocre choss piles of loose sandstone. However, it's interesting how you can take a flawless looking but shitty line up a stunning monolith, stir in some nearly unbelievable folklore regarding the epic of the well-known first ascent party, sprinkle a topo in a climbing magazine, add four or more stars after the name, and there you have it—instant classic.

Not known at all for its bouldering, I however had the inside dirt on the Secret of Sedona. A year prior, guzzling some double latte decaf espresso butt mud at the Kava joint in Bishop, I had a chance meeting with the near-legendary climber "Mad" Joe Jiminez.

For a human being, Mad Joe was a pathetic piece of work. With long scraggly hair, mottled skin, and the refined scent of an unkempt goat, he had both feet firmly planted in the cement boots of the 1970s, with no intention of ever removing them. Coincidentally, the 1970s were probably the last time he showered as well. But he was a great climber, gave great beta, and as I found out that day, he was also one incredibly nice human being. He'd give you the shirt off his back if you needed it, although you would of course refuse the rancid lice-infested rag. Just the same, it's the thought that counts.

As he tried to beg yet another cig and cup of yuppie coffee off me, I mentioned something in passing about wanting to check out the big red sandstone classics around Sedona. His voice lowered, and he moved closer to me. "Man, classic my skinny white ass, those multi-pitch sandstone routes are complete bullshit," he confided. "The ticket is the secret area called Boyton Canyon, man. Forget the Peabodies or the Happies; this place's got the best bouldering west of Hueco, and you got the whole place to yourself. Just some doped-up locals tripping on mescaline or peyote or some shit, wandering through the woods. But it's cool 'cause they're looking for a vision or something. They see you halfway up some V6, and they're all thinking you're Jesus or something. So you just go with it, like 'Yeah, man, I'm Jesus, now down on your knees and bow to your creator.' Ha ha ha! Feel the power!"

Two things struck me about his monologue. First, Joe was a well-known big wall slut, not known to lower himself to playing on the small stones unless under extreme circumstances—so these must be some fantastic boulders. Second, I found it hard to believe that there were classic boulders I had never heard of in Sedona of all places.

But I had to believe. Joe's enthusiasm was infective, like that of most hard climbers. Although their intentions are never less than admirable, hard climbers have a way of describing their morning stool in such vibrant, vivid detail that you can't help but follow them into the restroom to catch a glimpse of the masterpiece yourself. But shit is still shit, even with a spit polish.

His eyes glazed over like a college freshman watching hard core porn for the first time. Joe proceeded, like all humans known to be totally obsessed with the climbing way of life, to rattle off beta for several dozen boulder problems, complete with accompanying pantomime. I was already making a mental list of the problems I needed to tick, based solely on his verbal topo. In the end, after swearing me to secrecy, Joe left me with 12 squiggly lines and 15 word fragments scrawled in dull pencil on the back of my used cocktail napkin. This comprised the first known published guide to the Boyton Boulders. I carefully filed it away with the rest of my dreams and delusions, imagining the beauty of this place but never thinking for a moment that Mad Joe's "guide" would ever be used.

Yet there I was, about 50 miles outside of Flagstaff, again nodding off behind the wheel of my steel deathtrap. Several hours earlier, I had dropped off my sidekick Merve the Perve, having endured his annoying company during the inaugural segment of my climbing road trip to self-enlightenment. Now it seemed so right to be heading to this mystical place called Boyton Canyon, solo, and for a nice long stay.

Rather than bang my head against the steering wheel and power chug a twelve pack of Diet Coke in another futile attempt to stay awake, I opted for the chicken shit routine and pulled off the side of the road for some much needed beauty sleep. A few uncomfortable hours later, the sun poked its brilliant fingers of light through the windshield, prodding my eyes to open. Off to Flagstaff, then a stop in Sedona to buy supplies before beginning my search for the mysterious boulders.

There was still a moderate stash of microbrew in the trunk left over from my adventure with Merve, but it wouldn't hold me for the duration. I stopped at a small market on the outskirts of

Sedona to stock up. Between the magic crystals and ten variations of the "Guide to Vortexes and Other New Age Points of Interest" tourist maps, I found some hideously overpriced canned food, and a surprisingly decent sale on cases of Corona. Apparently, in a place where you get high for free off the cosmic energy, the beer is cheap. A bottle of Jack Daniels (purely for medicinal purposes) balanced out the essentials that should last for about two weeks of hermit-like bouldering, acetic eating, self-philosophizing, and vortex chasing.

An hour or more later, after pondering my ragged cocktail napkin and driving aimlessly along deeply rutted dirt roads, I chanced upon the obvious landmark Mad Joe had marked as signaling the primitive campsite. I parked and immediately ran northwest, and in two minutes found myself at the pearly gates of bouldering heaven.

It was breathtaking. The reddish soil and redder sandstone boulders contrasted heavily with the deep blue sky and the unusual bluish-green colors of the abundant junipers. The boulders themselves were eight to fourteen feet tall, heavily featured and just off vertical to slightly overhanging. Here and there, you could make out faint chalk marks. At this point I was smiling openly, as giddy as a virgin on prom night. I was beginning to feel the power of the earth as it shot out invisible columns of energy between the boulders, charging me up for an intense, extended physical and mental workout. I had been vortexed! I had been sucked into the cosmic toilet, like a human turd, beginning my metaphysical journey through the pipes that culminate in the ocean, coincidentally where all life began.

The rest of the day was spent setting up camp and familiarizing myself with my new, albeit temporary, home. The combination of the altitude, the energy I was absorbing from the vortexes, and my overindulgence of hoppy beverages made the place especially magical. I wanted to stay forever. And I had yet to touch stone!

The hours rolled into days, the days melted into weeks, and I was at peace. I soon fell into a wonderful routine. Eat a light breakfast of two Coronas, sunny side up, then head straight to the boulders. Boulder sporadically (the area is fairly spread out, limited to about 40 to 50 problems, mostly easy to moderate, but all of exceptionally high quality) and wax philosophically about existence and the meaning of life until mid-afternoon. Head back to camp for some "real" food and a nap. Late afternoon was spent drinking, and early evening was spent meditating on top of the highest boulder, surely one of the strongest vortexes in the area. After dark, head back to camp for a little more food and some hard liquor to ward off the demons of the night, and off to bed. No campfire. That might disturb the natural balance of this magical place.

For the first time in my life, I spent two weeks talking to nobody but myself. It takes a little getting used, when you're so alone that your thoughts pour out of your mouth like verbal diarrhea. Sure it's scary, but not nearly as scary as the overpowering smell of your own stench when you live your life as a full-blown hermit.

One afternoon, between pulling a V4 crimper face and cranking an overhanging V2 jug problem, I tried to imagine why Sedona was such a freak magnet. It probably started out very small, as most big things do. Somewhere in the past, a lone freak probably stumbled upon the place randomly. Maybe he was drunk, maybe he was stoned, or maybe he was just tripping on his own body fluids; but whatever the reason, he found the place especially cool. He went back and told a friend, another sort of freak, but a freak just the same, who was intrigued enough to make his own pilgrimage to the land of the cool. Before long, freaks from all over were converging on the place to do their freaky things.

A chill went up my spine as I realized the parallels between Sedona the new age capital, and Boyton Canyon the new bouldering Mecca. Mad Joe was the "first freak," and I was one of his followers. Before long, this place could be as crowded as Joshua Tree on a Saturday afternoon in April. All us wacked stone worshipers would come to Boyton to do our new-age stone worshiping, rubbing the big crystals with our callused hands. Behind our backs, people would laugh at us. But climbing was just the physical road we chose to travel to reach our ultimate spiritual destination. In the afterlife, your ape index is irrelevant.

And what of these vortexes, these focal points of invisible energy beams, these points of epic cosmic significance? I discovered their truth by accident one afternoon towards the end of my stay. Attempting to take a picture of postcard quality, I raised the disposable camera to my eye and maneuvered back and forth until the ultimate scene was framed perfectly in the viewfinder. After the "click," I looked down at my feet to see I was standing at the exact center of a circle made of stones. Smack dab in the middle of a vortex! So that was it. A vortex was little more than a scenic viewpoint with a new age stamp of approval. Yes, it was a focal point of cosmic energy, of sorts. But nothing upon which to base one's philosophy, religion, or life. Just a really pretty picture. After this discovery, the magic of the place seemed to lose a tiny bit of its luster.

Man is a social animal. While it's possible to learn a lot about yourself by spending an extended period of time in isolation, much of what you learn you were better off not knowing. The value of ignorance should never be underestimated.

It had only been about three weeks since I had quit my job and embarked on this journey. I didn't really expect to find all of the answers so soon, and my stay at the Boyton Boulders has provided little more than two or three of the pieces I'd need to complete this 1,500 piece jigsaw puzzle called life. But at least the pendulum was swinging in the right direction.

There was plenty of good bouldering to be had to the north, but I was in no hurry in my journey. The Hajj was now in full swing. No turning back. Time to center myself. To experience the raw energy of my own personal vortex in the Eastern Sierra, nature's answer to man's Stonehenge.

If I drove straight through, my raw fingers could be rubbing the magic crystals at The Buttermilks in a few hours...

The Stone Apocalypse
Episode Three:
Mr. Peabody's Traveling Side Show

This episode was first published on ClimbingChannel.com in 2000.

To me, The Buttermilks have always seemed to be a land of incongruities. You're in the Sierra, yet in the middle of a desert. Some of the "boulder" problems are taller than good-sized sport routes. The boulders lay amongst desert scrub, sticking out like a punk rocker at a bar mitzvah. You're at perhaps one of the best known bouldering locales in the world, yet in prime season it's not uncommon to have the entire place to yourself.

And where else can you climb a V6 boulder problem rated 5.10a?

After several weeks of bouldering in self-imposed exile in Arizona, I was starving for more than a little human contact, and quite ready for some over-socialization. Driving on a highway again was an interesting, practically unfamiliar experience. I found myself staring at the occupants of other cars, smiling broadly, almost insanely. They probably thought I was a recently paroled axe murderer, or at least a nut case. Maybe they were right. But I was enjoying their company all the same. They helped to make the drive up to Bishop pass quickly.

In Bishop, low on supplies and lower on funds, I raped my bank account as if my ATM card was some kind of deviant sexual torture device. Then off to the supermarket, where food galore filled my cart, then my car. Good lord, they even had a sale on Corona! My guardian angel, the patron saint of hops and barley, had accompanied me all the way from Arizona. With the money I saved, I splurged and bought two pounds of limes.

One last stop at the gas station to refill the tank, where I noticed a faded flier pasted slightly off center on a light post: the circus was coming to town! When? Who knows; my calendar-deprived existence made it impossible to determine what day it was, so I didn't even have much of a frame of reference from which to try. I suppose I could have looked at the date on the newspapers in the stands, or simply asked the clerk at the mini-mart, but that didn't make sense. It would spoil the fun. The day, the month, even the year no longer mattered. It was all just life now, flowing like a river; the goal would come, in its own time.

The Buttermilks or "Peabodies" are maybe half an hour outside of Bishop, but I planned to stay a while, not wanting to run in to town to re-supply every couple of days. The experience in Sedona had taught me I could survive such deprivation and isolation with relative ease. Before long I was at the sacred Buttermilks, setting up my primitive camp at my favorite spot, in the shadow of the Birthday Boulders. Then it was dark. The tent was there in case of rain or high winds, but as long as the weather held, the nights would consist of sleeping in the open, and drinking Mexico's finest while staring at the stars.

That first night, the flier from the gas station replayed a contorted movie in my head. I dreamed of Randolph, the Indifferent Circus Midget, and all of his side-show friends. They had heard I was a climber, living a life of Spartan decadence on the road, and instantly adopted me as a fellow freak of nature. Funny thing was, I felt strangely at home amongst them. They were my brothers.

If there was anything I learned from my trip to Sedona, it's that the universe is a pretty big place. A vast, unfathomable expanse of gases, ever expanding away from some invisible central point—a vortex, if you will. In fact, this could rightly be considered the grand pappy of all vortexes. We may never know the exact location of this universal vortex, and chances are it is nowhere near our solar system. But it couldn't be that great if every speck of dust in the entire universe was moving away from it at an unimaginable speed. Maybe the new-agers in Sedona had it all wrong. Maybe the point wasn't to gravitate towards vortexes at all, but to run like hell away from them. To go with the flow of the universe. After all, billions and billions of stars can't be wrong.

Contrary to the vastness of the universe, The Buttermilks were fairly finite. A set number of stones, and a new problem occasionally going up, made for a climbing area nearly as static as any other geologic phenomenon. The occasional earthquake of action was separated by long periods of near glacial inactivity.

The one dynamic at The Buttermilks is the steady procession of climbers who come and go. Usually not in large numbers, but a slow, steady stream; small handfuls of climbers, coming to this classic Eastern Sierra location to get their rocks off with mother nature. Maybe The Buttermilks wasn't a vortex at all. Maybe it was just a giant open-air circus, constantly re-staffed by an ever-changing assemblage of side show acts...climbers.

Dawn. Most people never really see it. To see it occasionally is cool; to see it frequently, to seek it out, can be magical. A climber might see it once in a while, when the alarm goes off at an ungodly hour and forces him into an early start up a long alpine route. But to purposefully wake just to witness the dawn, most people would label as a soft form of insanity practiced only by geniuses and fools.

Whatever. I had no intention of witnessing the dawn that morning. Unfortunately, that first morning, thinking I'd sleep in, I was awoken by the subhuman sounds of someone singing.

"Ding, dong, the witch is dead, the witch is dead, the witch is dead, ding, dong, the wicked witch is dead!" Praying for a moment that I was still dreaming, I awoke to the sight of "Mad" Joe Jiminez, hovering over my helpless body, his teeth missing and his dirty hair matted into dreadlocks by default, acting out his one man performance of The Wizard of Oz. When my lids separated and we made eye contact, he stopped in mid-strut.

"Ha, ha!," he exclaimed, "Good thing you woke up, man! I was just about to get down on all fours and do my Toto!"

"Joe...what the f@%k?" I asked.

"Yeah, I heard you were up here, man. Thought we could hang for a while." His face suddenly became very serious. "You got any beer?"

It must have been no later than 7:30 a.m. But time being of no concern on this voyage of enlightenment... "Sure, man," I said. "Corona. In the back seat. There's a couple pounds of limes in there too."

"Far out, man!," Joe said with authentic enthusiasm. "You've got more style than a nun at a leper colony." So this was how it was going to be. All right then.

Joe and I visited almost the entire day, and got quite drunk in the process. There was no climbing that day, just catching up. I went into exquisite detail about Boyton Canyon, a verbal tribute to Joe himself for turning me onto the place over a year ago with a dull pencil and a ragged cocktail napkin. Joe smiled so much that day, I was certain the corners of his mouth would rip open and his teeth fall out—at least the few he had remaining.

That first day, not climbing but wandering amongst the boulders, chatting with other climbing artists and watching them each apply color to canvas with their own distinct styles, I gained a much deeper appreciation for the climbing art.

That dream of Randolph, the Indifferent Circus Midget and all of his side-show friends would revisit me nightly, and haunt me daily throughout my stay. And over the course of my two weeks at The Buttermilks, I met a myriad of traveling climbers, many of whom were well qualified to work nights at a circus side show. The cast of characters changed almost daily, as few climbers considered The Buttermilks an actual destination like I had. And here I was, walking the same trails, climbing the same handful of boulder problems, nearly every day for two weeks. The only thing that kept me sane was the constantly changing human scenery.

And there was more to it than just people watching. I had initiated my road trip to find some kind of meaning. Having come straight off an extended period of solo bouldering and meditation in the woods, and learning a little from myself, I was ready to learn from watching others. Every climber is different, and every climber, regardless of age or ability, has something to offer the seeker. Every climber has developed his or her own personal philosophy, which can only be observed through a combination of watching them climb, and watching them live.

I learned most from watching others. I had come to The Buttermilks to again be with other people; not just any people, but climbers, who by their very nature are highly philosophical. By observing their actions, I could then pick and choose the pieces of philosophy that personally made sense, and reassemble them into my own custom belief system as we all do. Just because the resultant philosophy was not of cookie cutter perfection and shared by millions of others and blessed by a high priest of rhythmic joy did not make it any less valid. Each circus freak has his (or her) own cross to bear; their own idiosyncrasies, deformities, traumas. The Bearded Lady differs from the Queen of England only by a few bad genetic breaks and a little facial hair. One had to look no further than me and "Mad" Joe Jiminez to see that.

My tips were sore from repeated contact with the harsh stone, and my throat was parched from gasping for air on problems exponentially beyond my level of difficulty. At some point, not tired of The Buttermilks but keenly aware that my journey must continue, I knew my stay there was drawing to a close. I knew not yet where the road would take me the following day, but I would drink with my newfound friends of the day, and perhaps a destination would come to me in a vision.

I needed my medication badly, and reached into my left pocket for the key to my medicine cabinet—my Statue of Liberty souvenir bottle opener with the Ellis Island-shaped key ring. A brief pause, and I was instantly transformed into a man on death row, large electric shocks of disbelief shooting straight to my brain. Horror of horrors, inhumanity beyond belief—the bottle opener was not there! Miles from civilization, without an opener—with cans and twists-offs now the only available option, I was sure to perish, and probably wouldn't last the night. I frantically checked the pocket again and again, as if the fear breeding off my impending doom would somehow make the opener magically appear out of nothingness. But to no avail. Lady Liberty was gone, and with her my freedom.

Now I knew what it was like to lose a loved one. You go to the supermarket to buy some maxi pads and a fifth of Jack Daniels, and accidentally lose your son in the mayhem. In that terrible instant when you realize your child is gone, a twelve part tragedy unfolds before your eyes in a mere two to three seconds. You start to hyperventilate as the gravity of the situation hits home. Your life has been altered instantaneously. You realize you may never see your three year old child ever again. Your lifetime in an instant ends with a graphic scene of you on your death bed, in your eighties, having lived an entire life without knowing, and now dying in darkness, with no idea what ever happened to little Johnny. Was he kidnapped and killed 54 long years ago? Or was he raised to adulthood by another family? Did he grow up a criminal, or a doctor? Did he marry, have children? Were you a grandparent, maybe even a great-grandparent? What if things had been different, if you hadn't made that JD and maxi pad run that night, if you had just...?

"Dude, I found your opener in the sand," Joe interjected as he handed me my long lost son. Lady Liberty looked happy to see me, almost smiling, but her smile was nothing compared to the ivory I was flashing. As I opened the first of many Coronas that evening, little Johnny was immediately forgotten. Surely he would be happy with his adopted family, as I was happy with my temporary family of side show freaks. Meanwhile, I had some serious drinking to do, to help me forget the horror of those 30 or so seconds when I was alone on the planet without my bottle opener.

The sun took hiatus behind the Sierra crest, and we were left to amuse ourselves for the evening. The remaining members of Mr. Peabody's Traveling Side Show gradually assembled in a semi-circle; since no campfires were allowed, we all stared dumbly into the glowing eye of a gas lantern. The light was harsh and constant, not throwing the playful shadows that make an open fire in the mountains a source of endless nightly entertainment, but it was good enough for a bunch of freaks.

The beer flowed like a cool mountain stream, and we frolicked on the shore as our cerebellums waded deeply. The usual "No shit, there I was" climbing stories took form and rose above the group in a cloud of whimsy. Everyone was getting shit-faced. From his Navy issue overcoat, this dude we called The Captain pulled out a bottle of dark rum and took a long, deep draw from it. He then passed it around. Dark rum, from an oaken barrel stored below the decks of a tall wooden ship, delivered by a one-eyed, one-legged, scurvy-ridden mast-climbing sailor named The Captain. Aye, dark rum, a real man's drink.

The side show staff changed daily, as you would expect from an itinerant crowd of misfits each on their own never-ending search for meaning, but the mental snapshot of my brothers and sisters that last night at The Buttermilks was pretty typical of the days and nights I had witnessed throughout my stay. The names, faces, and other details were in a constant state of flux, yet taken at a courser level, nothing ever really changed all that much. This was the American dream, the climbers answer to the melting pot. Regardless of who was on the bill that night, "the show must go on." The actors were interchangeable, but the script was as static as a fixed line.

As the evening glided along, one by one the cast wandered to their cars and backpacks, and assembled a haphazard collection of pseudo musical instruments and other miscellaneous sound-making devices. There was Chewie the Werewolf, an incredible boulderer from the bowels of East LA, who got his nickname from his resemblance to Wolfman Jack. Chewie produced a set of well-worn bongos, which served the dual purposes of musical instrument and bohemian punctuation device.

Judy, or Miss Lovely as we called her, the hardbody blonde with her dark roots showing only on her unshaven legs, revealed herself to be above the rest by proudly displaying a fine banjo. Mohammed pulled a Jew harp from his back pocket. And "Mad" Joe Jiminez never went anywhere without his didgeridoo. Not being a very musical person myself, I simply picked up an empty Corona bottle and blew. In the heightened state of awareness the group was experiencing together, my noises meshed perfectly with the rest of the makeshift band.

Thus was the debut performance of Mr. Peabody's Symphony Orchestra. Various drunks took their turns at the invisible microphone, giving bad karaoke singers everywhere renewed hope at a Grammy nomination. We played all of the classic rock mega-classics, including "Smoke on the Water," "Freebird," something by Van Halen, and a Dread Zeppelin-inspired "Stairway to Heaven." The surprise of the evening was "Mad" Joe, totally out of character, giving a blood-curdling, dead-on rendition of Boy George's "Do You Really Want to Hurt Me." It was a thing of pure beauty. I was extremely intoxicated, and can't say for certain, but I swear I saw tears welling up in Miss Lovely's eyes as "Mad" Joe bellowed "Do you really want to hurt me?"

When and how it ended, nobody can remember with much clarity. At once it was both awe-inspiring in it's free form exploration of human diversity, and predictable in its representation of an ever-changing yet stable event. The morning after the big-top show, the circus freaks packed up their tents and left for their next destination. There would be countless other such performances in countless other places across the country, for untold years to come. The mix of players would change, but as sure as the sun will rise and the tide will recede, Mr. Peabody's Traveling Side Show will visit a climbing area near you soon.

I was off to visit another kind of side show, one designed by my own imagination. In the night, still inebriated, I had a dream. I was being chased by a big, fat, evil clown. His wig was the color of a grand Hawaiian rainbow, his feet were covered with floppy size 21 EB's, and his teeth were shaped like fangs. His name was Stinky the Armpit, and he was trying with gusto to steal my Statue of Liberty souvenir bottle opener, and attempting with great futility to use it to open 40 ounce twist-offs of malt liquor. He was chasing me along a paved road on the side of a hill, and at one point we passed the base of Borson's Wall. Thus, my fate was sealed. I must return to Southern California, even if just for an afternoon, in order to exorcise this demon clown. I would climb for the day with my old friend Max Armpet at Mt. Rubidoux.

The Stone Apocalypse
Episode Four:
The Malt Liquor of Bouldering

Portions of this episode were previously published in Issue #11 (March/April 1998) of mOthEr rOck magazine. The complete episode was first published on ClimbingChannel.com in 2000.

Part of learning, of growing, of becoming a better person, is doing things that don't particularly thrill you. It's about purposefully putting yourself into situations that make you uncomfortable, but serve a higher purpose. How else could you explain things like college, or a rectal exam? With this in mind, I decided to pay another visit to my least favorite classic bouldering area, Mt. Rubidoux. It was time to *do the doux*.

I had climbed at Rubidoux maybe 40 to 50 times over the years. At it's best, it was O.K. At its worst, on countless occasions, I left with such a bad taste in my mouth that I vowed to never return and to actually give up climbing altogether and take up needlecraft or even—gasp—golf.

It started with my very first visit there, back in 1990. This supa-fly climber with 10-inch forearms and a 12-inch ego traversed our toprope on the Triangle Boulders without even asking. He lifted our rope out of his way in mock disgust, fingers applying only the slightest of pressure to our lifeline, touching it the way your mom always did when she lifted your shit-stained underwear off the floor of your bedroom. Mr. dope-ass climber never spoke to us, never made eye contact, and never even acknowledged our existence as fellow climbers. He was, you see, too preoccupied with spewing to his spotter the good news, about how things were different for him, "now that I'm sponsored." Yuck.

No doubt Rubidoux is a very good bouldering area with some classic dime-edge problems that test your skills and force you to climb at a higher level, but the human element there can sometimes be as encouraging as an AIDS diagnosis.

I went back to Rubidoux a year after my first visit, determined not to let that one bad experience taint a potentially great local climbing area for me. It was different, but the same. A different cast of characters reading a slightly different script, but with the same prevailing theme: an elitist attitude. Off and on for 10 years, I had climbing experiences there that varied from mediocre, to bizarre, to downright bung water. I eventually concluded that if Rubidoux were a beer, it would be a big old 40 ouncer of malt liquor. It was good once in a while for a cheap buzz, but too much of it would lend a dank and foreboding tinge to one's very being. No doubt about it, Mt. Rubidoux was the malt liquor of bouldering.

On my way down from The Buttermilks to my next unknown destination, I'd spend a day living out my timid nightmare of Mt. Rubidoux.

I stopped at a liquor store and bought an extra large bag of Doritos and a few 40s of King Cobra, swung by Max Armpet's place to pick him up, and then parked it in the ritzy residential area at the bottom of the hill. The hike up seemed more strenuous than usual, but I was in much better shape this time.

It must have been mental. I was hiking up the side of the eroded hill towards the eponymous cross with my crash pad and malt liquor-laden backpack strapped to my back, and couldn't help but feel sympathy for that guy who, according to well-documented legend, had struggled up a hillside carrying a cross. The situations were entirely different, however. He was the son of God, on an important mission, and I was just a climber packin' my own body weight in malt likka. But it seemed like the perfect place to visit on a spiritual quest for bouldering nirvana, with the godfather of all religious relics mounted at its high point, the humungous holy lightning rod, a cast-iron Christian cross painted white, honoring St. Rubidoux, the patron saint of urban bouldering.

My climbing partner, or at least side kick, would be Max Armpet. For those of you who don't know Max, which is probably most of you, he is a big man in the Southern California climbing community. And I mean big. At 300 pounds and counting, it's a miracle he can climb out of bed, let alone up a shear rock face. Although an obnoxious human on many levels, and the singular inspiration for the new 5.4 slab problem I had put up a few weeks earlier at Boyton Canyon called *Fat People Smell*, to me he symbolized much of what was right about climbing. No matter what type of person you were, you could learn something from climbing—even if all you learned was that you were a big fat lard ass who couldn't climb.

Max was a virtual unknown in the Southern California climbing community, except to a few not-so-close friends, until he published the first in a series of self-depreciating articles in an issue of the late *mOthEr rOck* magazine in 1998. "I planned it as a series," says Max, "but I guess Matt (Artz, editor of the late magazine, and fellow heavy underachieving climber) got a bunch of letters and E-mails telling him what a funny piece of fiction it was, and to keep it up." Thus, Max had second thoughts about spilling his soul to an unsympathetic climbing community. "I spent my whole life being laughed at and not taken seriously. Why prolong the suffering?"

In the article, which appeared under the title "Confessions of a Lard-Ass Climber: Part One—The Formative Years," Max rambled on about how he achieved his lowly state:

> There I was. Run out four feet above my last bomber pro, about to clip into what appeared to be a brand new 3/4 inch bolt sunk deeply in solid rock, with epoxy liberally dripping out of the sides for good measure. I've never felt so helpless in my entire life.
>
> What's the problem, you ask? Eight feet is not usually considered runout, and could I have asked for a better bolt to clip?
>
> Well, you just don't understand. See, I'm a little different. My name is Max Armpet, and I'm a lard-ass climber.
>
> My story is one of hardship, trauma, indulgence, liposuction, and lost opportunity. Where do I begin?
>
> I guess it all started when I was born. My parents were quite hefty, and in the Armpet clan, I had large trousers to fill. And fill them I did. I was born with a silver spoon in my mouth, literally. By Elementary School,

they called me "Sumo." In Junior High, I had to stop wearing my favorite green (or "jade") colored T-shirt when the principal addressed me in a school assembly as "Buddha."

High School was no picnic, as I became the "butt" of the jokes of the rock climbing contingent; I was always invited on their outings, as pack mule and belay slave, only to find out later that it was all an inside joke, as the guidebook to the local toprope area stated "a large friend is useful for setting a TR." That one still makes my gut jiggle, even if it is at my expense. Shortly after graduation, I quickly dropped out of medical school when my academic advisor suggested for Christmas I ask my parents for a stomach stapling.

This was an important time in my life. At a loss for direction, I took stock of my situation. I had no job prospects, other than the fry machine at Mikey D's. Looking back, the closest thing I had had to "friends" in High School were those guys who used me for a laugh while climbing. It wasn't much to go on, but I had no life, so I decided to dedicate my life to underachieving as a full-time fat ass climbing bum.

The lifestyle suited me perfectly. My home became my Volkswagen Bus, modified to fit my bulky stature behind the steering wheel. It didn't leave much of a living area, but I didn't need much. To save room, I ditched the stove and lived off my own version of "power bars" (actually, any candy bar that's high in calories and low in nutritional value). Since the water at some of these places is often unpredictable, and since diarrhea is not an option when you have a swine's rear end and you don't shower for six months at a time, I drank nothing but piss-ant beer. This beverage served triple duty as it also helped me maintain my girlish figure, and when used liberally helped me forget my significant inadequacies as both a climber and a human being.

Not wishing to be the butt of any more "large friend" jokes, and not being able to find a harness of sufficient diameter to span my ever-expanding girth, I shunned all forms of roped climbing and started bouldering.

When bouldering low-ball problems and when lucky enough to find a partner for a few minutes before driving them away with my powerful personal odor and even more offensive personality, I learned to use the "power spot" in ever more creative ways. As my belly increased in size seemingly exponentially, my ability to attract power spotters with enough heft to support my manliness went the way of Lycra. I found that with a solid redwood 4 by 4 wedged between my ass cheeks, there was almost no 5.5 boulder problem I couldn't scale without a few solid days of work. With this third appendage sticking out like a mechanical tail, at Hueco they called me "Tripod." Well, some of them did. Most of them just said, "Hey, who's that fat dude with the 4 by 4 shoved up his ass?" No matter, though; I was making a name for myself at some of the finest bouldering areas in the Southwest, by doing numerous FFAs (First Fat Ascents). Bouldering purists like John Sherman won't appreciate my use of power spotting, but then what would Sherman know, that skinny little show off bastard. I hear John Gill did all his supposed first ascents years before he did anyway. All of the really hard ones at least.

Unfortunately for the masses, Max Armpet clamed up after that first shot at literary self-examination, and most of us would never hear how his story panned out. Unless, like me, you had the intestinal fortitude and/or bad judgment to get him drunk and go climbing with him. So it would be me, Max, several 40's of King Cobra, and the time-tested problems at Mt. Rubidoux, the malt liquor of American bouldering. I was already looking forward to this convergence of so-so cosmic proportions, this understated summit meeting between man, boulder, and barley.

To me, Max Armpet was the lowest common denominator, the last person you'd think of as a climber, the man with all the mental and physical cards stacked against him. But despite all that, he got out there and did it. Not to prove anything to anyone, not even himself. Just to get out there and do it, and have a good time at it.

The postscript to his article contained an ominous promise: "Coming Soon: Part Two—My First 'Epic'." But it wasn't meant to be. The self-depreciating humor of Max was lost on most readers, and Max was disillusioned with the underwhelming response to his confessional. Yes, that now-classic article in the lower-than-underground climbing publication called *mOthEr rOck*, once known for its low circulation and even lower standard of journalism, became a series of one. Max wrote no more. "It was the lowest point in a life known for its many low points," Max confided in me between violent gasps for air on the hike up Mt. Rubidoux. "That's when I found Christianity."

"Shit, it isn't Sunday, is it?" I asked, naively assuming that as a day of rest, Max wouldn't be allowed to do the strenuous things like climb and get loaded. And remember, in my temporally-challenged existence on the road, I had no concept of what day it was.

"No, man," he replied, "it's Thursday. Besides, it doesn't matter. Lately I've just been reading a lot of Neitzche."

This troubled me a little. College students usually read Neitzche when they go through the practically mandatory existentialist stage of intellectual development, which usually comes somewhere between the beer bong stage and the psychedelics stage. Point being, maybe Max was too old to be reading Neitzche. He was in his early thirties, and had never even been to college. He had been forced to learn about beer bongs and psychedelics the hard way—on the streets.

We arrived at the boulders as different as Abbott and Costello. After the steep Rubidoux approach, I was pumped, in good shape for climbing and other activities, all warmed up and ready to go. Max, however, was huffing and puffing like a spawning salmon, gasping for air in a futile attempt at sustaining life, his only hope for immortality being quick reproduction, which seemed highly unlikely given his advanced stage of lard-assness. The one thing we both had in common was that our packs were heavy with rock shoes and

154

multiple bottles of malt liquor, as we both planned on climbing on a higher plane that day.

"So, Max," I prodded, "wassup with the Neitzche? Last time I talked to you, you had found Jesus Christ. You not into that anymore?"

Max gave me a long, hard stare. He wasn't mad; it was more like he was wishing I hadn't asked that question, at least not so early in our day; like he had no idea how to answer the question, or even where to start. After an uncomfortable pause, all he could muster was "Man, that's a long story," as he took the lead for the first time and aimed his bulk in the general direction of the Beehive Boulder.

O.K., I'd give him a few minutes to open up. A few half-hearted attempts at *Beehive Crack*, 5.8, and half again as many pulls on his first bottle of King Cobra, and he started talking.

"You know, man, this whole religion deal is one big scam," he started. How's that for an opening line? There was enough in that one statement to outline the life's work of a team of ten crack apologists, but he continued with his philosophical jabs.

"You know those televangelists? They're the cream of the crop. But the guys who don't have their own TV shows—the guys busting their asses preachin' at the local church to a few dozen lowlifes every weekend—they're pretty good too. They're rehearsing on suckers like me, until they get their big Hollywood break—their own show. And that's all it is, man. God is nothing more than the big producer in the sky, pulling their strings."

Wow. So the "big man" had been burned by The Big Man! This was going to be more interesting than I thought. While he was confessing his sins, I had quietly knocked off *Beehive Mantel*, 5.10c, cranked that 5.11 face problem I always forget the name of, and done five quick laps on *Beehive Crack*.

"They told me it was O.K. to be fat. They accepted me for what I was. At first, it was so cool! I had never been accepted like that before, you know, like, unconditionally—not even by my parents. It was almost like it was too good to be true."

I took a pull or two off my 40, then we moved over to the traverse under the bridge, a nice sustained endurance 5.10+. I kept popping off towards the end, maybe because of the difficult crux move out there at the point of full pump, or maybe just because I was having trouble hearing Max when I was that far out from him.

"Finally, a group of people accepted me for what I was! I was fat, and it was O.K. to be fat! I had friends!"

Max took two more deep draws on his economy sized bottle of truth serum.

"But after a while, I started hearing them. They were talking about me, how fat I was. They were making fun of me, no different from everyone else. They talked a great talk at church, but they never wanted to hang with me socially. The acceptance was all a big act, like a cheap made-for-TV movie."

Was it Max talking, or was it the Neitzche? Neitzche, before descending the dark downward spiral into madness and premature death, was perhaps best known for his work "The

Antichrist," which was actually a bad translation from the German. A more accurate translation would be "The Anti-Christian," which is where Max seemed to be coming from.

"You know what the funny thing is? After all that, after years of just wanting someone to accept me for what I was, I realized something—I never really wanted people to accept me being fat, I just wanted to be thin. Their acceptance didn't matter, because I still couldn't accept myself as being fat. It's like I'm a thin person trapped inside a fat person's body, and I'm trying to get out. Why else would I climb?"

In my quest for climbing enlightenment, I knew the question of Christianity—the single most pervasive philosophical track chosen by my fellow Americans—would eventually come up. And here it was, handed to me early in the trip, stripped bare by the most unlikely philosopher of all—Max Armpet. Still trying to take in all he had said and make sense of it, I thought it was probably a good time to head over to Borson's Wall. Soon we were both sucking air—him from the short walk over to Borson's, and me from the bottom of my first 40, feeling fine, and fully entertained by Max's continuing rant.

This was what had started it all—my dream of Max the evil clown, bitter at not being accepted by society and driven to a hard life on the road as a white trash entertainer; chasing me in the shadow of Borson's Wall, trying to steal my precious bottle opener. Now, walking up to the base of Borson's with Big Max in tow, I was experiencing the ultimate case of deja vu, a reincarnation flashback of mind-blowing dimensions. Yet unlike the dream, this was the real thing. And in reality, Max was soon falling asleep under the rock, breathing loudly, his rolls of fat slapping over the side of my poor, lifeless crashpad like the love handles on a sumo wrestler. He wasn't evil; he was an intoxicated puppy dog. He wasn't stealing my precious opener; just my spot.

The combination of the unrelenting sun and the rapid ingestion of malt beverage was beginning to blur my vision around the edges and numb my senses in an ever-so-slight, highly enjoyable way. This was often when I did my best work. I quickly polished off the moves to *Borson's Face*, at 5.10a one of my favorite Rubidoux climbs. It had been a good four years, but the moves came back like the dialogue from a classic movie, dredged up from the depths of my memory, filed away with countless other lost memories until awakened after all those years when I happened to touch the same small bit of stone again with the same callused fingers.

"Man, I am so f@%ked up," Max loudly over-shared, not necessarily referring to the temporary situation he found himself in with the malt liquor, but instead hinting at all that was still wrong with his life, a deplorable situation he found himself in as a fat man in Southern California, Land of the Beautiful, Home of the Freak. But it was a situation he had created for himself, primarily out of over-indulgence and a lack of self control. Ironically, most of Borson's Wall is man-made, the classic problems randomly blasted out of the hillside with a few hundred pounds of dynamite to make way for the narrow paved road. As I moved my crashpad right along the road to protect me under *Black Pinch*, 5.10c, Max again sat on it and made himself comfortable. Obviously, he was a bit further along than me on his malt liquor tick list.

"I thought Christianity was the answer," he stated flatly as I pulled the desperate mantel at the top of "Black Pinch." "And it was!" he yelled violently, catching me off guard, almost causing me to blow the topout. "It was! Christianity had the answers—all of the answers, man, to all of my questions! To every question anyone will ever have! It was beautiful! While it lasted..."

I saw where he was going. I sat down next to him, unscrewed the top to my latest bottle, and gulped. For a fat man, he was deep. Real deep.

I couldn't help but draw comparisons between Max Armpet and Marco Vassi, who had so eloquently described his own short-lived infatuation with Christianity in *The Stoned Apocalypse*:

> It was as though lightening struck my brain. I saw how, in a single gesture, I could solve all the problems of my entire life, simply by putting all of my confusions in the hands of Jesus. It made no difference what my intellect thought of the matter, my emotion reined supreme. I jumped from my chair, grace pouring down on me from heaven.
>
> "I believe!" I shouted.
>
> "I'll have to give up my sophistication," I thought.
>
> "Your sophistication isn't worth anything anyway," Cheryl said, and I looked at her, amazed.

Within a couple of weeks, Vassi falls out of Christianity, with more of a whimper than a thunderclap, his soul undernourished.

"Yeah, that's the problem, man," I bullshitted. "Nobody has all the answers! If you've got all the answers, it's all just lip service."

This cat was striking a nerve with me. Here I was, at Mt. Rubidoux, in the shadow of the giant white cross that marks the high point of the mountain. What I was expecting from a day with Max was a fat man who would make my mediocre climbing look good; a man who would drink more than me, thereby making me look like less of an alcoholic; and heavy comic relief—a large butt of jokes, so to speak. Instead, I got an overweight philosopher with low self esteem, who was teaching me perhaps one of the most valuable lessons of my journey towards bouldering enlightenment.

On the way to Max's apartment in Riverside earlier that day, I had picked up a newspaper. After a few weeks of ignoring the outside world, I was interested in catching up on the news. To my surprise, the articles were boring and predictable, following a sad journalistic formula that did little to energize the paltry subject matter of international politics, mindless crime, and local traffic accidents. No, what enamored me most was the abundance of religious references. "Jesus Speaks Spanish," said one headline. Well, sure he did! Not literally, of course. Not in the "Buenos dias, compadre" sense. But he did. That truth was universal.

The way that religion had become woven deeply into the fabric of almost everything made me think that the rampant success of Christianity in America was perhaps related to it's ability to adopt and embrace and mesh seamlessly with elements of pop culture, especially the latest fads of the day. Christianity was the chameleon of religions. The failing of the common man. The lowest common denominator. The convenient answer.

Look at Christian rock music. Or the trappings of the evangelical, Born Again factions. And those little squiggly fish cartoons on many newspaper ads. Where would it stop? Maybe a signature line of "What Would Jesus Do" condoms? Christian cigars, Christian transvestitism, maybe even Christian porn? Who decides what an O.K. vehicle for Christian marketing is, and what is going too far? Invisible lines of moral demarcation are easy to cross when taken in small, incremental steps and shrouded in the haze of an overall environment of change. Like a borderline alcoholic abusing malt liquor on a day-to-day basis, the trouble was knowing where to stop. Before long, the many baby steps add up to one giant leap of faith, and the chasm is crossed between creative interpretation and fad-chasing blasphemy.

I was just coming to some monumental philosophical conclusion when my left foot skidded off a dime edge off the twelve coats of paint used to cover up such graffiti as "Jesus is Da Bomb" on The Block, under which there was supposedly a small hold a few decades ago. My methodical thought process concluded with a resounding "F@%k!" which echoed off the hillside.

Rubidoux often smells a little funky. Nearest I can tell, it's the smell of years of urine caked on the rock being baked by the hot sun, distilled down to an acrid chalky substance, which the wind spreads around the grass-covered hillside. And it seemed really hot that day, the sun beating down on my head like an LAPD baton on Rodney King's skull. Time for a little refreshment.

What role the charcoal filtering process plays in the yin and yang of brewing this white trash beer I'd never know, but who gives a shit. As smooth as paint thinner on a weathered fencepost, the liquid slid down my throat on the expressway to my brain. Halfway through the second 40, I remembered I was in a bouldering area, and had company.

"Do it, man," Max yelled in encouragement to some climber below us, just outside of my field of vision. "DO IT!" Yes, there were other people there that day, as I vaguely remember. The lone boulderers, risking their cajones for a chance to tick one of the off-the-deck dime-edge test pieces Rubidoux is known for. The gear-laden top-ropers, risking the wrath of hard-core locals for toproping the sacred solos, but just out to have some fun climbing. The non-climbers, hikers, partiers, gang members, homeless, and wanderers, risking a mugging, or there to perform one. Mt. Rubidoux, the melting pot of Southern California climbing—and other—cultures. Truly the malt liquor of bouldering.

Thanks to my previous bad experiences with Rubidoux, I avoided contact with these other folks as much as humanly possible. Why risk it? After weeks of bouldering in isolation in Arizona, I didn't exactly enjoy my own company either, but at least I could put up with it. And Max wasn't looking half bad at this point of inebriation.

I awoke in a daze, propped up against the rock, in the shade of a tree next to the Pepper Crack Boulders. My knees where scraped and bleeding from an obvious yet unremembered encounter with the rock, and my head was pounding. Eighty ounces—a lizard's bladder shy of a half gallon—of pure charcoal filtered satisfaction in less than an hour and a half had caught up to me like a loaded freight train hitting a brick wall head-on. I gradually came to, with Max blabbering on a rant, apparently oblivious to the fact that I had been unconscious and he had been speaking to himself for some time.

"Thas what we need, some wine!" Max blabbered. "Red wine. Just like the priests drink. Red wine. The blood of Jesus! A few bottles of that, and you'll be there, man. You and Jesus! The man! Thas what the priests do. You think they make that shit up? No, man, it comes to them in a vision. After they been drinkin'. Drinkin' red wine, my friend. Thas what we need. Where can we get us some red wine, Slim?" After a few moments of disorientation and the accompanying fear of slowly and painfully becoming familiar again with unfamiliar surroundings, I took inventory of the situation and was at least pleased to see that Max was more f@%ked up than me; I just couldn't hold my malt likka as well as he could.

His wisdom was fading rapidly, but so was my comprehension. It all made perfect sense to me then. Looking back later, I could see that he was just a drunk, fat fool. Like me, he was looking for the meaning of life, but he would have easily settled for a half hour with a cheap prostitute and a half gallon of cheap red wine. It was all about priorities.

What I was after on this trip—what everyone is after in their own personal journey to enlightenment—is to know the unknown. But the unknown can be divided into two distinct categories—the knowable, and the unknowable. Yes, to some questions, there are no answers. The sooner you realize that, the sooner you can get on with the important business of finding the answers to the knowable. To believe otherwise is pure folly on a grand scale.

Max and I shared more beer and philosophy back at his apartment, and in my heightened state of awareness, for the first time I saw him for what he really was. He was a man, like me. Inside, the skeleton was the same basic size and shape, made of the same raw materials. Outside, he just had a little more padding. The product was not bad in and of itself, but the packaging was poor, so most consumers weren't buying it.

Max also opened my mind ever so slightly to Mt. Rubidoux. Yes, it was host to some pretty cool boulder problems, and not all of the people there were assholes. Perhaps Rubidoux was bearable with the right company. And never had I imagined in my wildest dreams that Max would be the person to make me feel comfortable at Mt. Rubidoux. Maybe that was just the malt liquor talking, but it very well could have been true.

I awoke the next morning with much less of a hangover than expected, but my brain throbbed excessively from the intense philosophizing Max had subjected it to. We bid farewell, my fat friend and I, as I jumped in the car and headed up towards Idyllwild.

Adios, amigo.

The Stone Apocalypse
Episode Five:
Prodigy in the Pines

A slightly different version of this story was published in the Summer 1999 issue (Volume 3, Issue 2) of TopRope magazine.

Driving north on the 215, trying to shake the bad vibes of Mt. Rubidoux and the King Cobra migraine, I needed a drink—a real drink. The graffiti, malt liquor, urine-encrusted boulder problems, and my friend the fat philosopher had taken their toll.

A warm Corona rattled under the seat. I reached into my left pocket to retrieve the key to my personal salvation, my Statue of Liberty souvenir bottle opener. Under the crumpled parking ticket, on top of the 13 cents in loose change, between the four Corona bottle caps, and bonded to what remained of my expired drivers license, I found what looked like a well-chewed spit wad. What was this? I was about to toss it on the floorboard with the rest of the trash when... Oh, shit!

Like a Vietnam vet who hears the choppers and suddenly freezes in a futile act of mental self-defense, it all came back in a flash that left me shaking with maternal fear. It was a note from my mom. Crap. I could never find out the true meaning of life as long as I was distracted by that mental image of my mom shaking the rolling pin at me and chiding me for breaking the promise. I guess now was as good a time as any to take care of it.

In my late teens, I was living the great American dream of desperation: that of a middle class bum. Poised on the precipice between milking the last vestiges of high school and avoiding a job at all costs, there was this high school sophomore named Raul—an easy target for exorcising the demons I couldn't admit were inhabiting my own tortured mind. My mom and his mom slopped greenish meat product and pushed brown Jell-O for two hours a day at the high school cafeteria, making minimum wage and embarrassing their children to no end. I guess you could even say they were best friends. And although they never came right out and said it, they really wanted Raul and me to be best friends, too.

The problem was, Raul was a fag. Not in the normal sense of the term—he wasn't a homosexual per se, or at least there was no known shred of evidence to indicate an alternative sexual preference on his part. But that didn't matter. We were cruel youth, preying on the weak, and for some unexplainable reason, Raul didn't quite fit our demented definition of "normal." So like all "abnormal" youth, he was branded a fag and sent out to pasture with all the other lost souls.

Raul was subjected to all of the typical tortures and high school hi-jinx. For example, someone made up a rumor about him getting caught sniffing butt perfume off bike seats between classes. Highly improbable, yes, yet my friends and I did our part in perpetuating and even embellishing the unlikely rumor, in the process unwittingly elevating it to suburban legend status. In time, dozens of people claimed they had seen the Great Raul, King of the Faggots, set a new school record, sniffing 78 seats in between second (theater arts) and third ("homo" economics) periods—enough that his nose was supposedly chaffed to the point of bleeding, his head dizzy from the cumulative effect of the ass fumes. One guy even claimed he saw the entire incident written up in the Guinness Book of World Records—but less than half of the school actually believed this obvious distortion. Still, you occasionally saw a freshman hiding in a dark corner of the library, thumbing through the Guinness Book while mouthing "bike seat sniffing," hoping to verify the rumor and gain a better appreciation for the greatness of the infamous alumnus known affectionately as King Raul.

You can only hang in purgatory for so long. At some point, I actually pulled my life together, moved out, got a job, started climbing, and learned about "political correctness" —how, homosexual or otherwise, it was not nice to call anyone a "fag." Lesson learned.

My mom mentioned Raul from time to time; how he had had a difficult last couple of years in high school, enduring endless tortures both mental and physical from his less-than-tolerant classmates. I mocked interest with pursed lips and a furrowed brow, all the while repeating to myself in my best Beavis and Butthead impression, "huh, huh, what a fag." It was so wrong,

I know, but it's harder for shallow minds to pass up cheap shots than it is for the fat lady to forgo the eighth pass at the Sizzler salad bar.

Shortly before embarking on my road trip to self-enlightenment, mom told me Raul was interested in climbing. I could see it coming like a plane crash in slow motion. She made me promise to take him climbing some day, and neatly copied his phone number on a piece of paper. The same piece of paper which had now manifest itself as the world's most tightly bound spit wad, which I had so recently pulled from the motley assortment of life's odds and ends in my left pocket.

So there I was, on my way towards Idyllwild, knowing I was rapidly approaching Raul's home in San Bernardino, steering the car with the left hand while trying to unravel the spit wad with my right hand and my teeth, so preoccupied with my plight that the warm bottle of Corona still rolled around helplessly on the floorboards beneath my feet begging for attention. I openly prayed to all spiritual beings that cared to listen. I prayed the phone number had been rendered illegible by pocket rash; that this was really the wrong piece of paper; even that my veins would flow not with blood but instead with a nice cloudy Hefeweizen from the mighty Pacific Northwest. O.K., so this last one had little to do with the current situation, but I always throw that one in when I stoop to begging for divine intervention. Miraculously, the actual hand of God came down through my open sunroof and cleaved open the spit wad like a pistachio, revealing the puce green nut within. I could make out the phone number perfectly. Damn it!

With great anxiety, I dialed the number from the pay phone. I'd give him three rings, then hang up. At least I could tell mom I tried, and continue my trip with some semblance of a clear conscience. To my utter dismay, the former fruit picked up the phone immediately after the first ring. At least six years had passed since he was president of the drama club, and apparently he still had no life!

He was excited to hear from me. His mom had told him to expect my call, about six months before. "Uh, I've been busy..." My voice trailed off awkwardly, making it obvious it was a cheap, insincere excuse. Our conversation was brief and punctuated by many uncomfortable silences. I got directions to his place, which was only about three miles from the pay phone, and all too soon was standing in his apartment, making small talk with Raul Gomez, the man voted by his high school peers as most likely to date within his own gender. He was packed and ready to go. Thankfully, we worked out a plan where we would drive separately, with him following me up the mountain. I was careful not to give him detailed directions to the Relativity Boulders. In my last desperate plan to extricate myself from this adolescent nightmare, I would drive real fast and erratically, and maybe lose him on the freeway or something. Mom would understand.

Although I had been to the Relativity Boulders many times before, I had never bothered to read the "Speed of Light Experiments" plaque on the side of the road that gave the area its name. As if delaying the inevitable would make it a little easier, I walked Raul over to the plaque. A sick smirk crossed my face as I decided to perform my own experiments that day, my subject being not the speed of light, but the little rat named Raul.

I read the plaque slowly, mouthing the words. I paused for dramatic effect, read it again, and pondered its cosmic significance in silence for some time. Raul shifted uncomfortably, his eyes darting nervously from my face to the plaque and back again. I wasn't calling him a fag and offering him first crack at my bike seat, but I was winning the mental battle just the same. With great deliberation and a near-redneck twang, I exclaimed "Makes you think, don't it?" and then quickly turned and darted across the street and ran up the path to the boulders nestled peacefully in the pines. My little rat stood stunned for a moment, and then hurried through the maze to try to catch up with the amateur scientist.

Advantage: Slim.

As we sat next to the boulders to change our shoes, Raul pulled out his brand new Five.Ten Huecos, a copy of Craig Fry's "Southern California Bouldering Guide, Second Edition," and an obviously overloaded chalk bag with the price tag still attached.

"So, have you climbed much before?" I asked, knowing but not really interested in the answer. Instead, I was making mental calculations of how many cents on the dollar I would offer him for the pristine gear after I tortured him for a few hours on the boulders and he decided that his leisure time was probably better spent pursuing opportunities in community theater.

"Well, I saw some climbers on TV, and thought it looked really cool," Raul shared. "I saw it, and was like, 'Wow, that looks so cool, that looks like something I'd really get into,' like a total expression of my personality, because I love to try new things, take risks, do daring things."

As if. With my darkest sunglasses on, I could just barely make out the tag on the side of the Huecos. My size—cool! They probably retailed for about $100. But they were not exactly my style. I'd start with an offer of $10, and maybe go as high as $18 if pressured.

"I went to Sport Chalet and bought the shoes, and the chalk bag. I asked the guy where I could go climbing. He suggested this book, and explained about bouldering and the other kinds of climbing, but I really didn't understand it; he used lots of terms I'd never heard before."

Blah blah blah. The lips were moving, but I didn't really comprehend the sound. I already had a copy of the Fry guide, but could always use another one as a potential bartering item on this road trip—might be able to trade it for a couple beers at a dusty campsite far from a liquor store. $4, firm. If he balked, I'd feed him a line about how Fry was releasing the third edition next month, so his copy would be soon worth its weight in toilet paper.

"I only went out a couple times before, and didn't actually do any climbing. I couldn't find anyone to go with. I just took this book out to Mt. Rubidoux, and tried to find my way around. The maps were really hard to follow. I didn't know what to look for, how to figure out the climbs. I had no idea where to start. I'm glad you called. Climbing with someone who knows their way around will make it a lot easier."

When was he going to shut up? The price tag on the Black Diamond chalk bag said $14.95, and it was overflowing with fresh chalk. I didn't need a new chalk bag, but had always fantasized about wearing two—one for chalk, the other as a fashionable beer holder. O.K., maybe I'd give him five or six bucks, because it was an awfully pretty pattern and all, but I classified it as a luxury item and demoted it to the bottom of my post-torture wish list.

Sensing he was done spewing his life story, or was at least pausing for a moment to catch his breath, I quickly exclaimed, "O.K. then, let's do some climbin'!"

Sandbagging is such an ugly term, an act of cheap self gratification, demoralizing to your fellow climber in a way that makes you wince with pleasure. But since Raul wasn't technically a climber, and I had done much worse to him in my past life as a teenager, it didn't feel that bad. "We'll warm up here," I said, dropping my crash pad under a little 5.10d problem. I was cruelly dangling the cheese in front of my little rat. He had no clue.

First, a five-minute lecture on the basic elements of bouldering, Slim Roamer style. Body positioning. Friction. Dynamic versus static movement. Spotting. Crimping. Mantels. Falling. It was a jumbled mess of bits and facts collected over the last decade of touching stone, thrown out in random order at the unsuspecting victim, part of my twisted little experiment that was half Sigmund Freud and half Hannibal Lecter. I was no teacher, for sure, but he appeared to eat it up.

Enough talking; it was now time for a hands-on demonstration. I mounted the boulder, which has some tricky feet at the start and a semi-dynamic move to the lip then a fairly straightforward mantel. In less than four seconds I was over the top.

Raul trotted up to the boulder, naively intent on simply repeating what he had watched me do just seconds earlier. Yet he couldn't even grasp the holds. After a few tries and a few pointers, he was able to grasp the initial holds, but couldn't get his feet established. As I did the problem a second time for instructional purposes, his frustrations began to show.

"I have to get this," he said firmly. I had never seen such intensity in him before. Maybe he wasn't the same meek little seat sniffer I had known in high school. Or maybe this was the way he always had been, it's just that I had never seen past the cruel mask I had played a part in lacing over his face. "I will get this."

I left Raul to repeatedly throw his body violently against the boulder while I did other problems. From time to time, when moving from one boulder to another, I would walk up and ask him how it was going, even throw him a few more pointers. In between attempts, he sat cross-legged on an adjacent boulder, his eyes firmly fixed on the problem at hand as if meditating. The look on his face was one of total concentration and sheer determination. As the afternoon progressed, he became ever more intense. I suggested that he try something easier, but he refused. "I *will* get this," he repeated, quickly dismissing me and my suggestions. I left him alone with his nemesis.

The name of the classic problem *Robin Hood* at the Relativity Boulders always made me smile. In this idyllic little community of tidy vacation homes tucked away in a virtual Sherwood Forest, Sir John Long and his band of merry men came and liberated the privately held land. They borrowed it from the rich landowners and lent it to the poor—the partiers, the beer guzzling rednecks, and the dirtbag climbers. Sometimes, if you came up late on a Friday or Saturday night in the summer, you might even get lucky enough to stumble across Robin himself, hiding in the bushes, his pants around his ankles, Maid Marion on her knees giving him one for jolly old England.

I floundered on the first five or six moves of Robin Hood, with all the grace of a spawning salmon, and finally resigning myself to the inevitable. All bouldered out, my gills gasping for air, I took a few minutes to regain my composure and then went back to check on Raul.

As I rounded the corner, I nearly ran over him. He was breathing hard, seemed three inches taller, and the look on his face spoke more than he ever could with mere words. "I got it, man!" he exclaimed. "I got it!" I congratulated him, and we sat down to share my bottle of water.

It was too easy to let petty jealousy lessen the greatness of his accomplishment. Besides, I got over it after about 5 or 10 minutes. I then proceeded to explain in all seriousness the gravity of his achievement. A personal recollection of how incredibly long it had taken me to do my first 5.10d boulder problem. Stories of other climbers and their more gradual ascent to success. And the mandatory "it's more than just numbers" speech, which sounded even more lame to me than it probably did to him. Still, that smile was superglued to his bespectacled little face, and it wasn't coming off any time soon. He knew. And he knew that I knew. Everything else was just smack.

Walking back to our cars, neither of us said anything. I looked over at a familiar boulder, and again heard the choppers of distant memory circling overhead.

One time at the Relativities, alone, I had come across the mother of all rattlesnakes. I had the entire place to myself, and I watched the snake as it half hid under the side of an overhanging boulder. It was that day I realized I had never really heard the famous "rattle" the species is known for, despite numerous encounters with the feared reptile over the years. Nobody was around. I'll throw a stick, and hear this thing once and for all.

The first stick landed two feet from the snake, which remained completely unfazed by my lame projectile. Innumerable attempts followed, some landing closer, some even further from the target. The only thing remaining constant was the snake, frozen solid, as immovable as the stone behind it.

With renewed determination, my tenth or fifteenth stick arched through the pines, finding the perfect line. The final stick struck the snake like a hammer on the Berlin Wall, and the resulting sound was heard round the world. Like a Rain Bird on PCP, the snake rattled as if possessed by Satan himself. The sound was nearly deafening, and although alone, I cowered behind the trees with authentic embarrassment and then quickly ran back to my car. Sometimes one should leave experiments to real scientists, lest the rat—or rattlesnake—turn around and bite your amateur ass.

Back at the cars, we shook hands, exchanged a few pleasant words, and for the first time in my life, I envied the scrawny little boy I had spent my youth calling "fag." I taught him a little about climbing, and he taught me a lot about determination and will power while helping me keep my promise to mom. I had helped awaken the rat within, and it was now up to Raul to keep it fed. From what I had seen, it wasn't going to be a problem. My prodigy in the pines would be climbing 5.13 in no time.

Advantage: Raul.

Taking Back America
Reclaiming the Birth Stones of Our Fathers, One Carabiner at a Time

Originally written for Vertical Jones but never used there, this story appeared in Issue #2 (Winter 99-00) of FunPig magazine, Issue #30 (Winter 2000) of What's the Beta?, and on ClimbingChannel.com (2000).

The two lights danced across the parking lot, their dull orange glow revealing the failing batteries powering the headlamps, their erratic movement hinting at the exhausted state of the climbers behind them. But these climbers carried no secrets. They'd be the first to admit they were exhausted. For they had just done a classic Yosemite big wall in a day. A very long day.

An unlikely team they were. Two excellent climbers, who had never climbed as a team until that day. They had met thanks to a chance posting on the Internet, discovering a common desire to push the standards of the day in the Valley.

Alfrinio, the Spaniard, and Günter, the German, limped and grunted, bobbed and weaved their way through the parking lot, trying in vain to find the rental car they had left early that morning before the sun rose.

Suddenly something caught Günter's eye — not the car itself, but something, well, out of place. His headlamp illuminated the sparkling pavement, a glistening carpet strewn across the otherwise unlit parking lot. He froze momentarily, then slowly panned his dying beam upwards, revealing a car, a broken window, and...

"Fook!" he screamed, their common language of English distorted by his heavy Germanic accent. "Our fooking car!"

Meanwhile, at a ramshackle campsite in the historic Camp 4 made famous by climbing heroes like John Long and Jim Bridwell, two climbers of the new era inventoried their booty.

"Six hexes, three Aliens, nine assorted cams, one decent rope, a stove, two nice down bags, one water filter, assorted toiletries, and a kick-ass tent," Dick Claiborne reported. "Not bad for two minutes of work!"

"F@%king Germans," said Sammy 'Chock' Smith. "We're takin' back America. Right, Dickie?"

"Shit yeah," replied Dick. "It's our f@%king country, man."

"Yeah. Now let's go get something to drink."

The bad boys of Camp 4 shared little in common with their now-famous predecessors. Dick was a wanna-be veteran, talking constantly of Vietnam, but obviously too young to have served there. Chock was an alcoholic; not that Dick wasn't also, but Chock's insobriety simply showed a much higher level of commitment. On the evolutionary scale of alcoholism, Dick was just slapping the mud with his flippers, while Chock had long ago learned to walk upright and fashion crude stone tools.

For some reason, Dick was the captain, the man in charge, the big Kahuna. Perhaps it was due to his overbearing personality or his imagined position of leadership in the military, or maybe it was just that Chock was too worried about where his next buzz was coming from to give a shit about Dick's power trip; in the end, Dick was always the master, and Chock the puppy dog lapping at his heels.

Their modus operandi was a combination of big talk and petty theft. While Dick liked to think that America in general and Yosemite Valley in particular were being ruined by European tourists, don't let the climbing rhetoric fool you. He in fact was driven by the same motivations as most small-time thieves. He was a lazy man, looking for a quick fix to his own problems, and using imagined greater societal problems as a weak scapegoat to make something bad seem almost decent. At least Chock was honest to himself. He went along with Dick's anti-European rant as long as it kept him flush with petty cash for brew and the occasional weed.

In the summer of 1992, life was good for our anti-heroes. Dick was reveling in his power; a born leader, he contrived some sort of gear thievery on an almost nightly basis. Chock was in a near-constant state of being f@%ked up, a binge so long it was threatening to exceed the one he had while employed as the night clerk at his uncle's liquor store down south in Diamond Bar until he lost that perfect gig after a long-overdue inventory was conducted and 43-odd cases of malt liquor turned up missing.

The many non-European climbers cycling through the campsites at Camp 4 were ecstatic over the excellent deals they were getting on slightly used gear. But Dick was feeling less and less satisfied. "This is sweet," he told Chock. "This is real sweet. More gear than we know what to do with. Enough money to buy us a nice dinner every night, and more than enough beer. And best of all, we're teaching those f@%king Germans a lesson, right, bro?"

"Yeah," Chock replied from behind a thick sheet of fog. "F@%king...Germans."

"Damn straight. But I been thinking, Chock. Sure, we got us a good thing going and all. But what are we really doin'? We're f@%king up a few Germans here and there, but what are we really doin'?"

"Huh?" asked Chock. "We're, like, livin' the good life and, uh, takin' back America, ain't we, Dickie?"

"Sure, man," said Dick. "Sure. But I mean, what are were really doin', in the greater sense of the word? Are we...ah, f@%k, you just don't get it, do ya, Chock?"

"Uh, no," replied Chock, "I guess not."

"O.K., let me put it to you this way: we need to do something big. Something real big. I got a plan..."

When dumb people have a streak of dumb luck, they sometimes get a false sense of intelligence; they then do something so dumb, so blatantly stupid, so comically asinine, that even the slower people in society stand back for a moment and say "What the f@%k was he thinking?" Had Dick been honest with himself, he may have noticed the futility in his plan. And had Chock been sober for even a few hours, he probably could have pointed it out as well. But alas, it was not meant to be. A half-baked plan mixed with half a brain yields a slim chance of success.

Dick had been scoping out a victim since the early morning. Three Swedes, or "f@%king Germans" as he liked to refer to them, had left about 2 a.m. laden with heavy haul bags, in the direction of Half Dome. He would set fire to their vehicle, shooting a glorious flame into the sky like the torch on Lady Liberty herself. "Just like the f@%king Fourth of July," Dick told Chock with glee.

Late that night, Chock watched carefully from the pay phone across from the parking lot. As he stood ready to dial the number of park police and trying to remember the script Dick had written him about taking America back from the Germans, Dick popped the gas cap off the Swede's rental car and slid a piece of shiny cloth down the fill tube. He waited nervously for the gas to soak its way up the torn shirt sleeve, for what seemed like ten minutes but was probably only about thirty seconds.

Chock saw the spark of Dick's lighter, then the dull flame. Then nothing. Then the spark, the flame, and darkness again. Must be the wind. Chock took a long swig off his 40 ouncer, savored the charcoal-filtered aftertaste, and watched the scene unfold.

In fact, it wasn't the wind that was the problem; Dick was having trouble getting the makeshift fuse to light. Maybe it was some kind of cheap foreign polyester blend, he reasoned, having remembered that the original garment was lifted about a week prior from the car of some f@%king German tourist. "Wouldn't have this trouble with 100% American cotton," he mumbled under his heavy breath.

At some point, Dick realized that the real reason the flame wasn't taking to the shirt sleeve was that the gas had not soaked all the way up to the end of it. How much more did it have to go?

What followed was Dick's downfall. In one blinding flash, his own stupidity cheated him out of the glory of his perfect plan. And Chock had a ringside seat. As Dick naively positioned both the lighter and his right eyeball close to the fill pipe in an attempt to judge the level of fuel left in the vehicle, there was a loud bang. Like a flame-thrower in the Vietnam of Dick's imagination, a shaft of fire shot out of the gas tank more than 20 feet. Chock dropped the dime for the pay phone and instantly forgot his carefully scripted speech claiming responsibility. "HOLY SSSHHHHHEEEEIIITTT," he screamed, the corners of his mouth turning upwards and forming a slight smile. All he could do was stand back in awe, clutching his 40 of malt liquor tightly as Dick rolled across the parking lot attempting to quell the flames coming from his upper body.

Park Service firefighters watered down the smoldering remains of the Swede's rental car as a park ranger led Dickie to the car in handcuffs, his face blackened, eyebrows gone, and hair still smoking. His run was over. All that was left now were the memories.

"We took back America, didn't we, Chock?," Dickie yelled across towards the phone booth. "Didn't we?"

But Chock was long gone. He had finished his 40, and was already back at the ice chest in the tent for another round.

www.ingramcontent.com/pod-product-compliance
Lightning Source LLC
Chambersburg PA
CBHW030335030726
47499CB00003B/782